For Samuel Menashe

THE PAPER TRAIL

from

a "fan" and friend,

A Recollection of Writers

Dorothea Straus

THE PAPER TRAIL

A Recollection of Writers

Dorothea Straus

MOYER BELL

Wakefield, Rhode Island & London

Published by Moyer Bell

The author gratefully acknowledges the following publications in which parts of this book first appeared: "A Chuckle from the Grave" in *Shenandoah* magazine; "Little Colette" and "In the Medici Woods" in *Partisan Review*; "Women's Studies" in *Confrontation* magazine; "Across the Tiber" in *Raritan* magazine and "The Americans" in *Commentary*. Thanks to Houghton Mifflin for permission to reprint "The Culture Professionals," "Two Gothic Profiles," "The Road to Mandalay," and "Götterdämmerung" from *Showcases*, and "Many Mansions" and "The House of Letters" from *Palaces and Prisons*. Thanks also to George Braziller for permission to reprint "Singer's City" from *Under the Canopy*. The following chapters first appeared in *Virgins and Other Endangered Species* (Moyer Bell): "Demons and Supernatural Presences," "The Heraldist," "A Voice from the First Generation," "Epitaph of a Modest New England House," and "The Letter Writer."

First Edition

**LIBRARY OF CONGRESS
CATALOGING-IN-PUBLICATION DATA**

Straus, Dorothea.
     The paper trail : a recollection of writers / by Dorothea Straus.
— 1st ed.

          p.   cm.
     ISBN 1-55921-195-4
     1. Straus, Dorothea—Friends and associates.   2. Straus, Dorothea—
Biography.   3. Women authors, American—20th century—Biography.
4. Publishers' spouses—United States—Biography.   5. Authors and
publishers—United States—History—20th century.   6. Literature
publishing—United States—History—20th century.   I. Title.
PS3569. T6918Z474   1997
813'.54—dc20
[B]   96-31207
                                                                                                    CIP

Printed in the United States of America.

Distributed in North America by Publishers Group West, P.O. Box 8843, Emeryville, CA 94662, 800-788-3123 (in California 510-658-3453), and in Europe by Gazelle Book Services Ltd., Falcon House, Queen Square, Lancaster LA1 1RN England 524-68765.

With thanks to my husband, Roger Straus, whose publishing house provided me with most of the models for the impressions found in this book.

CONTENTS

FOREWORD

The portrait sketches of writers on these pages are various, joined only by the books they have left behind along a paper trail into the future. Yet the endurance of their reknown is unpredictable—which will last longer, the name of Edmund Wilson, Colette, Isaac Singer or Mary McCarthy? Will some obscure author be discovered posthumously at another day? No one can answer these questions with certainty.

For the sake of order, I have placed my subjects under two headings: *On Home Ground*, and *Abroad*: Americans who wrote in their native language, Europeans, translated from French, Yiddish and Italian. There are, however, a few who evade this clear-cut classification, and in accordance with my own view, I have located them among foreign colleagues.

Although their work is the posterity of the artist, I am more concerned, here, with my encounters with the men and women, themselves. Each one has been quickened by the vagaries of personal recall and I follow where it leads, thankful for fleeting victories over the erasures caused by the inexorable passage of time. In a sense, memory is the protagonist in this book.

ON
HOME
GROUND

Chapter One

THE CULTURE PROFESSIONALS

The meaning of "culture professional" is not to be found in the dictionary. By my definition it is someone who promotes the arts, which, in turn, enhance his own status. Money, talent, charm, brains, political or social power may be used for this purpose. Although the culture professional is a manipulator, he is also frequently a benefactor. For me, Stanley Young and his wife, the writer Nancy Wilson Ross, were archetypes out of my past, encountered along the circuitous route of accident and circumstance.

What is left for me to remember of the war years? Scraps of souvenirs glimpsed between the piled bricks of day-to-day living: newspaper headlines that implanted in my consciousness such heretofore unknown places as Iwo Jima, St. Lô, Guadalcanal, Anzio Beachhead; the familiar, sedative voice of the newscaster over the radio, making household heroes out of the names of MacArthur, Patton, Stilwell—resplendent for their brief span, like Fourth of July rockets, before subsiding into past glory. Today I am returned in time when I hear the siren proclaiming a peaceful noon. It is the same sound that used to announce air raid practice—a warning, followed by an all-clear, conjuring up images of gas masks like nightmare elephant trunks, and shelters under city streets ready to offer claustrophobic hospitality to the beleaguered.

There was the summer weekend my husband (on leave from the Navy) and I spent at his family's fishing retreat in upstate New York. The murmurous river was soothing, and so were the mingled smells of dry pine and hay and the sight of the trim white house with its red shutters. But the small clearing in the woods and the heavy heat were oppressive, and, far off, the war was continuing on its relentless way. I sat in a garden rocker on the flagstone terrace above the river, surrounded by pots of geraniums under a candy-striped awning. I was enjoying the sight of my husband in tall waders, his fishing rod over his shoulder, his creel filled with trout, as he climbed nimbly up the embankment toward the terrace. At the edge of the clearing, Mr. Ertz, the farmer, was plodding back and forth from the barn. Like the hot summer weather, there was in Mr. Ertz a submerged threat. His healthful outdoor existence was marred by the horror stories he delighted in telling. He would often pause in his chores when he spied me, idle, on the terrace. "Just heard that the Maples's cow gave birth to a three-legged calf," or "Awful motor accident down Bearsville way, car wrecked, everyone killed." His thin-lipped, colorless face would remain expressionless, but as he picked up his pitchfork or pail he seemed to derive new energy from the discharge of another calamity. I watched him walking steadily along the path and as he drew near I felt the latest news, like an ugly herald, going before him. I pretended to be reading but it was useless; he was standing close to me, pushing his battered felt hat back from his perspiring forehead, holding his silence a moment longer for effectiveness. Then, "Heard over the radio, we just exploded an atom bomb in Japan—destroyed a whole city and everyone in it. No one has ever seen the like—." His burdens made lighter by the delivery of another disaster—the summer sky darkening and the rumble of thunder announcing the approach of a storm.

In war as in peace we are, for the most part, selfish and egocentric, and the climax of the war for me was my husband's tour of duty in the Pacific. As the day of departure drew near, threatened, he became once again the dazzling stranger I had married five years earlier. He appeared more handsome in his blue and gold ensign's uniform, more desirable, never to be taken for granted. When he had gone, flying toward some distant island—tropical, evil, erupting—I felt abandoned, perched high in our apartment, unhomelike in its loneliness, with my infant son, a responsibility grown heavy because I was alone. The nursery was sunlit, overlooking the reservoir in Central Park where the changing light recorded the hours of the day. One afternoon, a friend came to see the baby with her husband, a lieutenant who had just received orders for combat in Europe. I can still re-create the scene: the bright nursery, papered yellow and white with a lighthearted frieze parading around the walls, the baby in his crib and the visitors bending over it, admiring him. Is it hindsight that makes me see the young lieutenant, rosy cheeked, curly haired, in his new infantry khaki, within a bower of light more brilliant than the sunny nursery? It may be—because he never returned. He was killed in the Normandy invasion, and he has left behind in my memory that last picture of him by the side of the crib, his scrubbed, snub-nosed face illumined like an image in a medieval book of saints.

I can recall little of those long weeks of separation. Occasionally, a letter from my husband reached me. Although I would read it many times, the words were disappointingly inadequate, but the thin airmail paper he had touched had value. I lived with a constant sensation of helpless anxiety, the threat of falling victim to the churning public events. I tried to drown fear in small household duties. But when I looked at my son, my heart would often lurch heavily, for he too might be a sacrifice. And it seemed to me that childhood was pathetic, even more vulnerable, ignorant, and hopeful than the adult world. I watched the baby taking his first steps and my happiness was feigned. I wanted my husband to share the moment, to guide the teetering attempts around the chintz cliffs of the sofa and to right the tumbles on the wide terrain of the living room carpet. And all the while I had the feeling that it was I who would never learn to walk alone.

One morning, as though directed by radar, I made the discovery of writing. Here was the antidote to anxiety; a world that I could order, an escape from the treacheries of the day. With the aid of memory, I was empowered to resurrect a sleeping past and bathe it in the varied colors of my own imagination.

I wrote a story and it was quickly finished, and then quickly forgotten with my husband's return. I remember the airport filled with men in uniform. The arrival of the awaited plane stopped my breath with joy and awe. I was caught in the toils of the giant supernatural bird, blinded by its dazzling wings and deafened by its uproar. When it settled to the ground, I strained to identify my husband among the small humans being disgorged from a hole in its side. Where had they been? What had they seen? At last I spotted him, his uniform creased, his black hair rumpled, his sun-burned face looking tired. And I noticed that, oddly, he was wearing the scuffed house slippers I used to know next to the bed. Later, I learned that this was because he had cut his foot on a coral reef. But at the moment of arrival it seemed an intimate, loving gesture, a reassurance that our separation and the intervention of so many miles, alien places, and experiences had not, after all, made him a foreigner to home and to me.

The war in the Pacific ended as I was listening to the news one night on a summer porch. The announcer's voice was accompanied by insect wings making their tiny barrage against the screens and by a chorus of tree toads croaking all around us in their dusky green hideaways. The European war was over for me with even less emphasis, and with indecent haste its memory dropped away. Only the sight of a young paraplegic in a wheelchair, the upper part of his body aglow with animal health and strength, his unrelated legs wasted and useless, was a reminder—or meeting a wife and mother for whom family life was not resumed. I tried to hold on to the exhilaration of reunion and the relief of security, but they too slipped by in the midst of my treasuring.

One day when I was clearing out my desk drawer, I came across the story; it seemed to me, now, in another life, written by a different person. It lay valueless among old invitations, checkbooks, stamps, and discarded snapshots of the baby. Yet with a kind of stubborn loyalty to the fulfillment it had once afforded me, before burying it with the rest of the trash, I gave it to my husband to read. "It's good," he said. "I'd like to show it to Stanley Young. He's one of the best younger editors in town, and a poet himself, besides." In this roundabout way, Stanley Young and his wife Nancy were introduced into my life. And I entered theirs through the stone gate posts that led into the flourishing acres of The Orchards, the Long Island estate of the Wentworth family, that provided the Youngs their fastness against the world.

I suppose that Stanley had pronounced his approval of my writing before that first visit, because my entry at The Orchards is accompanied in memory by a new awareness of accomplishment that radiated through me with the stimulating warmth of fine spirits. And as I stepped across the threshold, though uncertain, I felt at once the embrace of this new world, as the most insignificant choir boy partakes of the pageantry of the church, and, though far below him, is yet germane to the ultramundane person of the priest. At The Orchards, a priest and priestess officiated jointly. The Youngs lived in the gatehouse to the estate. It was ordinary enough from the outside, made of gray shingles with a covered veranda leading to the door. But once within one was enveloped by the strong odor of incense, and it was so dusky that only a shaft of bland Long Island sun lit up, here and there, a strip of Chinese calligraphy hanging on a wall, an enigmatic stone figurine of the god Shiva, or a single rosy-tinted spray of orange blossoms that seemed as weighted with meaning as the Cross.

Stanley and his wife greeted us. He was a tall, springy man, with a shock of tawny hair and a virile, ruddy pioneer's face. Only his eyes, of an intense blue like the tips of flame, hinted at a connection with the spiritual world. His words might be bluff but his glance seemed to be saying, "You and I are special—we do not belong to the world of Philistines." He was dressed in a turtleneck sweater and tweedy jacket, more indigenous to the paddocks, and game rooms of The Orchards than the modified sari and long ropes of Oriental beads worn by his wife. She, too, had a mane of tawny hair and, although she was short, hardly reaching her husband's shoulder, she gave the impression of greater strength. She was beautiful, with large, dreamy amber eyes, so wide-set that they seemed to be looking in two opposite directions at once, toward the disparate cultures of East and West whose threads she blended on her person and in her home like strands woven from an invisible loom. At the time of our first meeting, Nancy and Stanley were newly married, but they seemed already to be a team guarding in mutual understanding the sacred premises of the arts and admitting only the select through the doors of the temple.

The visits to The Orchards merge in my memory because of their sameness, differentiated only by the revolving seasons. In the winter the Youngs and their guests remained indoors, ensconced in the Bauhaus chairs and sofas. These chunky free-form pieces had a dated look, like popular flappers grown ungainly in their middle years but still considered audacious. Nancy had studied in Germany at the Bauhaus when she was young and her furniture was the inheritance of those times. On the walls were Oriental paintings, attesting to her enthusiasm for Zen. She was the author of several novels that subtly combine her American roots with an Oriental cast of mind. And her learned books on Zen have the kind of intensity that only an outsider can bring to an alien culture. She presided among her collections and her guests with a connoisseur's pleasure in their worth. The guests were of various ages and belonged to all the arts. They came and went, but a hard core of wealthy Long Island and New York socialites remained. Always present was Priscilla, born a Wentworth and married to a Yugoslav journalist. An actress, she was the daughter of the owner of The Orchards, and in her quiet way a rebel, having refused to be presented to Long Island society. She preferred the world of the theater and the Youngs gave enthusiastic support to this preference. She dressed in sandals from Greenwich Village and dirndls from Austria, and with her flaming hair, proud bones, and white face she reminded me of a smoldering Hester Prynne. Stanley would sit casually, boyishly at her feet or at mine. But his attitude was never subservient; rather, it was masterful, combining the omniscience of a priest or guru with the natural flirtatiousness of an attractive male in the presence of a young and admiring female. "Are you working?" he would ask, and his flame-blue eyes would bore into mine as though reading there the record of my many derelictions. I felt that he saw and disapproved of my walks in Central Park with my son in his baby carriage, the parties I attended, the weekends at our country home—all of my conjugal life. These were my sins—and with his long legs folded tailorwise, his hair becomingly tousled, his ruddy plowman's face turned up to mine, Stanley Young played father-confessor, drawing out my transgressions and forgiving them simultaneously. "Oh, the world is too much with us," he would say, "we must flee, we must shut ourselves away; for the artist, work is the only salvation."

I was by nature an outsider to this monastic utopia recommended by the Youngs, but their inclusion of me was flattering and stimulating. I would watch Nancy poring over a Japanese print, exclaiming at its fragile beauty and explaining its occult meaning. Sometimes she would look up with a sigh and softly take up her husband's refrain but with a greater emphasis, "Yes, the world is monstrous. It is our duty to protect ourselves." And at The Orchards I always did feel protected but exalted too, with that amorphous thrill experienced during the moment of silence before a great performer strikes the opening notes on the keyboard.

When the weather was fair, the Youngs would stroll with their guests over the spacious grounds of The Orchards. Although they were only tenants, living rent-free in the Gatehouse, they seemed to be the true lords of the place. At the end of winter we would find the snow melting in porous patches beneath the great old trees that, in summer, had cast patterns of leaf-dancing shade over the mowed and watered lawns. The swimming pool was encircled by a ring of Buddhas which, even transported from so far away, looked at home at The Orchards. However, their sleepy stone faces above the clear aquamarine of the water seemed to be issuing a warning from the ancient, static wisdom of the East to the heedless, enterprising West that their jewels were dearly bought and transient. As we walked around the flower gardens, the orchards, the tennis courts, and the paddocks, Stanley would bend down to pick up an early autumn apple from the russet and green carpet beneath the bountiful trees. "Still sour," he would say after one bite, and hurl it with athletic speed toward the invisible horizon of the acreage. Or Nancy would pluck a single white rose from a formal bed. "It's too lovely! A perfect creation," she would murmur in prayerful contemplation. It was hard for me to believe that the Youngs had not always been part of the place, that he had sprung from Indiana's parched Corn Belt, that she had begun life in the Northwest in Olympia, Washington. Perhaps it was from there that she had first directed her wide and brooding gaze towards the mysteries of the Orient.

Sometimes we would visit the main house, a conventional Georgian mansion which, after the war, when we were introduced to it, was inhabited by Austin, the youngest Wentworth, and his pretty wife Melissa, with their brood of children. Austin's sister Priscilla would spend the weekends there with her family when she was not detained by a theater engagement. The beauty of Priscilla and Melissa ("Prissy" and "Missy," to the Youngs) was as romantic as the heirloom portraits of bygone wives and mothers of the family adorning the walls of the house. Priscilla's and Melissa's shining hair and correct features were as lovely as the Lowestoft chain, Chippendale furniture, mirrors, brasses, and artful bouquets that surrounded them. And they were as well cared for. But Priscilla was robust and blooming, while Melissa was delicate, bedridden at this time with a touch of tuberculosis contracted when she had been a nurse's aide during the war. Her lingering illness was a reminder of the harsher war days, now quickly disappearing from our memories like the patches of melting snow under the trees outside. Melissa Wentworth would be sitting up in her high four-poster bed when her five children would be brought to her by an English nanny and her subordinate nursemaid. Melissa would languidly pass their beauty in review, one by one, but at the entrance of the Youngs her face would light up with admiration and trust.

"Look, Missy, I have brought you this perfect rose," Nancy would say, offering the bloom as though it were her own creation.

Nancy's interest would frequently be diverted to the nanny, her apprentice, and their charges and she was on intimate terms with all the Wentworth servants, calling each one by name. She deeply savored the Old World regime of the big house, and I imagined that her vision repainted the scene in the delectable colors of a Fragonard, a far cry from the abstractions and the Chinese calligraphy at the Gatehouse, but in contrast perhaps all the more alluring—for everything is enjoyed as a relief from something else. And I was also certain that all this was raw material for the Youngs, eventually to be transformed in the expression of their own work. That Stanley and Nancy were artists the Wentworths never forgot either. And like the Medicis before them, their generosity was amply rewarded by the presence in their midst of these birds of rare plumage.

I remember especially one hot summer evening in the Youngs' living room, the mercury hovering close to one hundred degrees, the nights bringing no relief but the cessation of the sun, all the more suffocating, like being buried alive in a dark hole. Nothing stirred outdoors; the guests sat in an expectant circle on the Bauhaus furniture, for Stanley was about to read his long poem in progress: *America, My America*. I can recall some of the faces. Timothy was the rebel scion of a conventional, wealthy Boston family, who lived most of the time in a pink villa on the Riviera, endlessly writing the memoirs of his homosexual expatriation. Elsie and Charles Johnson were there—she had been Nancy's classmate out west. A chirping, elfin woman, interested in textile designing, she had married, moved from Greenwich Village to Sutton Place, and dutifully produced an heir, and I felt that Nancy considered her a defector to the Philistines. The Johnsons, however, were usually included in these gatherings. Then there was the usual assortment of aspiring writers for whom Stanley, in his role of editor, was guardian and inspiration.

I observed him closely as he glanced through his manuscript before starting to read. As usual, he was sitting on the floor as though taking part in an undergraduate get-together. There was something unusually attractive about his virility and plowman's handsomeness, especially when one knew that it was the outer covering for the soul of a poet. He reminded me of the prince in the fairy tales who had been bewitched into the body of a bear.

"Shall I begin?" he asked, looking with pleasure around his circle.

I do not remember much about *America, My America*, but I can still hear Stanley's rich voice with its trace of midwestern pronunciation, reading on and on, and feel the wicked heat that locked us all in feverish quarantine. And I can see Nancy spread out on a sofa, dressed in diaphanous Indian gauze of turquoise and gold. The robe swathed her body ceremoniously without seeming to touch it, like the tent of a rajah. As her husband read his poem, a few tears trickled from her large eyes.

I was stirred by the familiar feeling I so often had in the company of the Youngs. It was a combination of my admiration for them and their way of life and the faint stirrings of unrealized possibilities in myself, like an adolescent's first awareness of physical love, a future experience he promises himself, something at once sweetly personal and grandly universal. From far off, I realized that Stanley had stopped reading. Everyone was silent. Then, Nancy, wiping the remaining tears from her eyes, exclaimed, "Can you believe that this man is still a white-collar worker? How I have implored him to leave publishing! It is my mission to see that he shuts the door on the world, once and for all, in order to write, write, write—."

Stanley did in fact retire from publishing, and his charm has been employed instead on the boards of art councils and foundations. He travels around the country disseminating culture and his still boyish resilient personality. I do not know whether he has ever found the time to complete *America, My America*. Nancy has grown more involved with Eastern philosophy, writing books about it and lecturing. After each trip to the Orient she returns still more adorned with Indian, Japanese, and Thai silks and jewelry, more inwardly withdrawn than ever from the "monstrous" world we all live in. She is still lovely but has grown stouter, and her amber eyes look disillusioned now rather than dreamy. "The group" has been dispersed: Priscilla, divorced and moved to San Francisco; the young Austin Wentworths and their children are in Washington. The big house is empty and Nancy and Stanley have lost contact with the nannies, sub-nannies, parlor maids, and butlers who once graced the airy, polished, flower-filled rooms. The use of the Gatehouse, however, belongs to them for life and they are free to wander over the well-tended but deserted grounds.

It seems to me that the balance between artist and patron is in constant flux. On an invisible seesaw, money and the arts take turns: once Stanley and Nancy Young were up, now in many places it is wealth that plays host to culture. This occurred to me one night as I wandered around the immensity of the lobby of the New York State Theater during an intermission of the ballet. Gold was everywhere, as far and wide as the eye could reach. Tiers of golden mesh rose to the lofty ceiling and the small dark silhouettes of the crowd looked like prisoners in a bejeweled Sing Sing pacing their golden-wired cells. Downstairs two gigantic white sculptured figures stood sentinel. Their immobile size, dominating the scene like a double version of the cemetery statue of the Commendatore in Mozart's *Don Giovanni*, presided over the gala exhibition—the explosive interplay between a plethora of wealth and talent.

The public event that first brought to my attention a changed note in the age-old duet of writer and patron was the inauguration of John Kennedy. On television millions witnessed the new President taking office. It was a cold day in Washington, and Kennedy, coatless, looked youthful and vital. As he spoke, his warm breath made puffs of vapor in the icy air. His guest of honor, the poet Robert Frost, appeared as old as Father Time himself. Shrunken inside his heavy wrappings he stood close to the small brazier that was unavailing against the sharp winter's day, and he recited his poem in a voice as feeble and intermittent as the faintly smoldering coals. The President's voice rang out with clarity and hope; he was the all-powerful host. Despite his obvious reverence for the age and genius of his guest, they reminded me as they stood side by side on the television screen of a crowned monarch and a wandering minstrel brought before him for his entertainment.

The salon of Winifred Root is another illustration of the workings of a wealthy culture professional. Through the door of her town house, renovated beyond recognition for her by a famous architect, pass the illustrious in all the arts. On her "evenings" she is to be found seated at the center of her brilliant circle, a massive woman as ponderously immobile as the sculpture that fills her rooms like a petrified forest. The stark white walls are hung with paintings by her protégés. Those unrepresented are scornfully referred to by her as "passé." Winifred receives in long medieval robes of costly brocade or velvet. She is past middle age and her cropped wiry hair is graying. She has the even features of a Roman emperor, and a bulging high forehead, and she continually mops her brow with an inadequate scrap of lace handkerchief as though she were helplessly overpowered by the electric vibrations of her inspired guests. Yet in her salon she is queen and the performance at her command.

A Mexican poet has been reading his verse—rendered in English, also, by a translator. The poet is dressed like a prosperous businessman in a black pinstriped suit. He has a large head, swarthy and bald, and his eyes are as inscrutable as a Buddha's. His translator, a professor of Spanish from a midwestern university, is wearing a peasant blouse in homespun fabric and sandals. The Mexican delivers his poetry with passion—it is a call to arms, an invocation to a hidden Power. When he pauses, everyone is quiet until the hostess breaks the spell. "It's just too much! I shall be ill from emotion," she exclaims, mopping her expansive brow. She has, indeed, turned red and apoplectic as though she had siphoned the fire of the artist into her own veins, a difficult and painful procedure achieved at great expense and at the risk of shattering her delicate sensibilities. "Encore, encore!" she cries bravely.

The poet is reading his latest work, *My Country*, and I am reminded of Stanley Young and of his and Nancy's court in the Gatehouse—the Chinese calligraphy, the single blossoming branch, the Bauhaus furniture, the smell of incense. Through the rolling cadence of the Mexican poet I am seeking the special intimacy of Stanley's voice, so long ago, reading *America, My America*. I feel a moment's resentment of change. But perhaps nothing has changed very much and I am regretting my own inability to strike gold dust from the scene. And that magnetic tandem, Stanley Young and Nancy Wilson Ross, was it in part my own creation, the result of an earlier, brighter vision?

Chapter Two

THE HOUSE OF LETTERS

On the first visit to Wellfleet on Cape Cod the summer following Edmund Wilson's death we found the house the same yet strangely altered. His widow, Elena, ushered my husband and me into the wing that had been Wilson's kingdom consisting of library, bedroom (once a woodshed and added in recent years during his illness), and bathroom. In the library not one volume had been disturbed. They were well cared for, yet they looked dim and recessive. The low-ceilinged and meandering book-lined workroom, once the heart of the house, had been abandoned. Taine, Proust, Michelet, Tolstoi, Chekhov, Pushkin, Dostoevski, Gogol, Turgenev (the latter in the original Russian), Dickens, Renan, Balzac, Dante, the grotesquely erotic drawings of Aubrey Beardsley, and Fuseli—philosophy, history, literary criticism—all Wilson's lifelong friends stood faithfully in place on their shelves.

Light filtered from a corner window near the desk. Over his work chair a sign in Hebrew read: "Let us be strong, stronger still stronger," a chant used by Talmudic scholars exhorting further efforts. Wilson had come across the lines while doing research in Israel for *The Dead Sea Scrolls*. A stuffed owl bearing an uncanny resemblance to Wilson was now the recipient of the ancient message. And in the village cemetery just beyond the house a simple tombstone under a great shade tree is engraved with the same phrase. As it had accompanied Edmund Wilson, alive, now it seemed to be following him in death. We were aware that the temerity of our toothbrushes in the bathroom, our open suitcase packed with bathing suits and jeans in the bedroom, and our appropriation of the adjacent library would not transform this wing into guest quarters. The absence of a presence barred the way.

My introduction to the Edmund Wilsons and to the house in Wellfleet took place in 1950. Of that visit nothing remains but the recollection of sitting in the little flower garden situated outside the "blue room," always especially Elena's. On this August afternoon we were awaiting the arrival of Edmund Wilson, who was in Boston for the rehearsal of his new play, *The Little Blue Light.* My husband had just become his publisher and I was eager for this first meeting. At that time Wilson was in his late fifties, but I imagined him already venerable, indelibly etched against his reputation, an American Gibbon or a Samuel Johnson. I pictured him like a central character out of Molière, an intimidating eccentric seated center stage with his bandaged gouty foot upraised, surrounded by a group of minions ready to execute his every testy demand.

Elena Wilson came from an aristocratic European background: a German father, heir to the von Mumm champagne fortune, and a White Russian mother. Her childhood had been divided between a formal town house outside of Frankfurt, and hotel suites in Paris and Switzerland, and it was punctuated by visits to international resorts fashionable around the time of the First World War. After Hitler's takeover she had left Europe and her family, arriving in the United States, armed with the courage and idealism that would continue to serve her through the years.

In her New England garden that looked like a multi-colored apron attached to the early nineteenth-century Cape Cod house, she was far removed from the *hôtels splendides* of Biarritz, Davos, and Marienbad. Yet now she belonged here. I observed her; a tall woman, slightly stooped, her posture reminded me of a stem, flexible but resilient. Her face was lovely and blooming. She looked more Teutonic than Russian: casual bobbed wavy blond hair, gentian blue eyes, rosy skin somewhat weathered from the salt air of her adopted land, a sensitive nose with flared nostrils, and a generous mouth, slightly puckered as though she were about to laugh, cry, or pronounce one of those German words that require oral calisthenics. But French was Elena's first language and she spoke the correct English taught by governesses, tinged with a foreign inflection. She was wearing a faded checked gingham shirtwaist dress, her sunburned legs were scratched from berry picking and dotted with mosquito bites, her large solid feet were bare. Yet there was about her an air of regality. The Wilsons' two-year-old daughter, Helen, playing near her mother, had been born when Elena was over forty and Edmund twelve years older. The baby was sturdy, with features already firm and determined. She regarded us with owlish omniscience. There were other children by the Wilsons' previous marriages. We were discussing a forthcoming book of collected essays, when Elena broke off to exclaim, "Edmund is approaching!"

I kept looking down the country road that ran close to the house the occasional passing automobile did not stop. At last I asked, "Didn't I hear you say that Mr. Wilson was arriving?"

"Oh, he won't be here for another forty minutes."

"But I thought—"

"I only meant that I felt his presence," she answered in her deep voice with its foreign inflection. "I know these things. I have a kind of sixth sense—" This was said quite simply as a statement of fact. A touch of other-worldliness completes my first impression of Elena. Contact with the mystical was as natural to her as the company of the crowned heads of Europe must have been to her parents, vacationing at summer spas or winter ski resorts.

Edmund Wilson did indeed arrive at the minute predicted by his wife. But that initial meeting is unclear in memory, as though I had been trying to discern him through a glare—projected not by the "blue light" of his own drama but by Elena's extrasensory prologue to his entrance on stage. That afternoon belonged to her; after that Wilson generally took over. And I never again set foot inside the small garden attached like an apron to the blue room. It became a picture behind a glass door: a daguerreotype, idyllic but flat, a background against which we were posed for an instant: Elena, Helen, my husband, I, and that blurred likeness of Edmund Wilson—the progenitors of our later selves.

In many New England country houses the kitchen is situated so that it constitutes a central gathering place. The Wilsons' confronted the visitor as soon as he entered the door. In all seasons we lingered there in informal sociability around the perimeter of the oilcloth-covered table on which Elena would have placed a jug of rambler roses, zinnias, autumn leaves, or a sprig of pine. She was an early riser, moving about downstairs at daybreak, and when we descended, the ashtrays in the kitchen would already be filled with the stubs of her morning cigarettes. She was a proficient but absent-minded cook, plodding back and forth between range and table, her feet still bare, her scrubbed face devoid of make-up.

Now Edmund Wilson entered the picture. He would appear later, sometimes still in pajamas that had an oddly formal look. Elena would serve him a special meal in her distracted but efficient manner—pancakes or Irish oatmeal—which he ate with appetite while delivering vehement opinions on the Russian novel, new and old—or extolling the fascination of a language he was currently studying: Hebrew, Russian, modern Greek, or Hungarian. My portrait in advance had not been altogether incorrect. In his fifties Edmund Wilson did look old, but in a crusty solid fashion that one felt would be more lasting than mere youthfulness. For the twenty years I saw him, a few times each year—until his final illness—he did not change. In the beginning I found him intimidating: his snappish comments, his talent for utter silence that was even more disconcerting, his explosive laughter that sounded as though it were erupting over obstacles, like a dammed waterfall forcing its way between heavy boulders. In the morning he joined us around the kitchen table, but he was the unmistakable potentate. He would at times unbend with my husband, who could call forth most frequently that eruptive laugh, and Wilson's faith in him, blunt but unswerving, endured. In his bathrobe and pajamas he did resemble that cranky eighteenth-century character I had anticipated. Short and plump, his presence was nonetheless impresssive, his face owlish, his features grown smaller in proportion to the expansion of his jowls. He had round, protruding, claret-colored eyes under hooded lids—the eyes of the perpetual scholar most at ease when cast down upon the page of a book. Yet when he raised them to the world about him, nothing escaped their reddish brown stare. His nose was pointed and inquisitive, his mouth above several chins was compressed, more censorious than his eyes. His hands were small, doll-like, as though belonging to a lesser man.

My husband and he would have much to talk about. Later in the day when they shut themselves into Wilson's study, Elena and I would go for walks along the beach, accompanied by the current Wilson dog. The first, addressed by Edmund as "old flea-bag," had been a furry mop of uncertain shape and breed. He had been succeeded by "Brown," for the most part, boxer. In November, the dunes were like bare giant shoulders exposed to the chilly crystalline glint of the sea and a flawless blue sky. Our footprints were insignificant on the expanse of smooth sand and Elena's ease alone with nature communicated itself to me.

In the early days lunch and dinner were taken in the dining room. Later, when Edmund was ill and Elena's burden had increased, the kitchen served for all meals. The dining room was conventional American Colonial but Edmund, ceremonious in the observance of holidays—anniversaries, Easter, Christmas, birthdays—not even overlooking April Fool's and Valentine's Day, had contributed ornaments that stood out in the homespun décor like orchids growing among wildflowers. I remember, in particular, an epergne made of mauve frosted glass that might have graced the salon of one of the hostesses of Marcel Proust.

I rarely entered the adjacent drawing room. It was obscure, furnished with authentic American antiques: a black horsehair sofa, a maple desk honeycombed with caches, a table covered in green baize. This room did not seem to belong either to Elena or Edmund. It was the departed spirit of Mary McCarthy, its former mistress, that lurked in the dusky corners. An authentic New England drawing room, correct and quaint, it might be prized by an outsider from the raw Northwest.

In the Wilson home, the guest bedrooms are reached by ladderlike stairs. White-painted wooden doors are still bolted by the original iron latches the floor and ceilings tilt at dizzy angles. The rooms are numerous but small and unadorned, but the windows hold pleasant segments of rural views: a white-shingled extension of the house topped by a weather vane, a patch of tangled field, an old oak, the narrow rugged dirt path separating the main house from the crooked front steps of the "cottage."

Everywhere there was a trace of salty dampness and the nostalgic smell of old country houses: a mixture of recent scrubbings and the unmistakable residual odor of longevity, as though soap and water had been joined to ineradicable dust and rot. All the extra bedrooms were repositories for a copious overflow of books. Here, stacked on hand-built shelves, bureau tops, night tables, and window benches, were to be found the leftovers of bygone research: the Depression years, Indian tribes of upstate New York, Russian literature and the Russian Revolution, the Civil War. Their bindings rubbed shoulders with discarded review copies and the works of old friends now outmoded: Dawn Powell, Waldo Frank, Louis Bromfield, Zelda Fitzgerald, Dorothy Parker, Sinclair Lewis, John Dos Passos. In this setting they, like the odor in the guest bedrooms, had an antiquated lure.

Many hours were spent in Elena's sunny "blue room." Perhaps I thought of it as hers because of its color that complemented her eyes in a symphony of blues ranging from royal to delphinium to pale cerulean. I was mesmerized by a small painting on the wall: A wooden door opening on to the dunes and a clear sky, executed in minute detail, it appeared to be a real aperture in the cozy room, as actual as the garden beyond the glass door. Elena would curl up on the powder blue couch. At night she would be wearing a long loose blue robe, her bare feet tucked up under its hem. Edmund ensconced himself in a certain armchair nearest the entrance to his study. In the "blue room," he always seemed a visitor, albeit an illustrious one. His conversation dominated. At these times Elena was mostly silent, but her bright blue eyes were lively and her generous mouth always appeared on the verge of laughter, crying, or pronouncing that tongue-twisting German word foreign to the rest of us. Edmund's monologues, like his mirth, were spasmodic, delivered with a slight stammer that added emphasis. His face would grow suffused in apoplectic red, brought on by his vehemence and by the succession of drinks that marked the evening hours with the steadfastness of the ticking of the grandfather's clock in the unused drawing room.

Other visitors were rare. Sometimes Helen, now a teenager, was there with a group of friends. Elena kept casual open house for young people who were drawn to her. She respected their point of view and they admired the unself-consciousness of her youthful spirit. Edmund remained obdurately the "grand old man." He held himself aloof from his children and their companions, but I am certain that no detail escaped the observation of his hooded eyes. From his chair, clapping his doll-like hands, he called out imperiously, "Bring in the hippies!" And Helen and her friends would troop into the blue room, court jesters for his entertainment. The girls wore floor-length printed cotton skirts, T-shirts over free-bobbing breasts, and handmade dangling jewelry. They looked like Gypsy fortune tellers. The boys, long haired, in picturesquely patched jeans, resembled Greenwich Village saints. College students and dropouts, they consecrated themselves to crude carpentry and the baking of coarse whole-grained bread. Helen's features were bold and clear-cut; she had heavy bones and large gray eyes like the women from Picasso's "classical" period. But her expression, honest and penetrating, was her father's, and her young lips were molded in the shape of his eloquent severity. Harlequins on parade, Helen and her friends presented themselves before Edmund, and like Old King Cole, enthroned on his chair, he passed them all in review. The solemn humorless "generation gap" had been converted into an extravaganza: a clash between the exuberance of youth in confrontation with the self-respecting authority of age.

The blue room contained portraits and snapshots of

Elena's family: her granddaughters by the son of her previous marriage, her mother pompadoured or in a large hat trimmed with milliner's roses, wearing a boned high-collared shirtwaist or draped in a boa. Of Edmund's family there were no pictures. It seemed to me that he carried his heritage and traditions on his person. Behind his intellect that had penetrated in wide arcs so many foreign places and people stood the indigenous New Jersey and upstate New York Calvinist ancestors—shadows stubbornly clinging to light.

In recent years some new paintings had made their appearance on the walls of the house in Wellfleet. Angular, uncompromising portraits and bright still lifes—they were the work of Helen Wilson. Last spring my husband and I dined with her in her studio loft, the size of a skating rink, in New York City. But her paintings stood out undwarfed. There were self-portraits without a tinge of prettiness. Helen's classical features caught in moods of cool detachment, and likenesses of members of her circle of friends, also painted without mercy, magnified heads against grounds of brilliant patterns. I recognized the paintings of goblets, eggs, sugar bowls, shells, vegetables, and fruits that I had seen before in the house at Wellfleet. In the stretch of the loft-studio a dining table, some miscellaneous borrowed chairs, and a bed were reduced to insignificance. Helen was wearing a burlap robe, and with her straight Joan of Arc hair she looked like a priestess. This was Greenwich Village 1975 and it occurred to me that history in its circular fashion was repeating itself. Helen had the leading role that evening in a situation recalling the one enacted years earlier by the young Edmund Wilson, caught up and converted by the lure of the arts and of free love in the Village circa 1920. After dinner, consisting of a quiche, a loaf of home-made black bread, plenty of red wine, and a salad culled by Helen from the stalls of Chinatown, she brought out some old family photographs for us to see. Among them was a wedding group: The bride and groom were Elena's parents surrounded by a large formal gathering in front of a home whose dimensions and glass port-cochère entrance vied in opulence with Berlin's Hotel Adlon. The groom was wearing Elena's face and the face of her son. He was tall and slender and also stooped like a stalk in the wind. Everyone looked long-lasting, yet they were all dead now. The photograph had found its way to this Greenwich Village loft. Helen's guests, the young harlequins, gazed in amazement at the richly dressed, pompous figures. Yet, mysteriously, Helen, one of them, was also connected to that buried scene. My husband and I bid good night to our hostess and descended the clanking iron stairs, seven flights to street level. A gentle rain had begun to fall. The grimy sidewalk littered with trash cans was deserted, but I felt companioned by the phantom of the young new-Bohemian, Edmund Wilson, and the members of that wedding party. The American writer and the offspring of the European bride and groom, widely separated, innocent of their fate, were to be joined at some future point through the intricate weavings of chance and time.

Between Boston and Wellfleet an early winter blizzard had begun and soon we were shrouded in layers of cotton batting. Our rented car crawled and skidded on the deserted highway. Now and then the twin glow of headlights, seemingly detached from any vehicle, approached us out of the horizonless universe. Nature had triumphed and the airport we had just left had grown remote in time and space. When finally we arrived Edmund and Elena gave us warm welcome. The snow was flattering to the old house, a study in white and replacing the noise of cars (on what used to be the country road) there was a dense hush.

But inside the library we found a real haven from the

storm—or perhaps, its ally, because here also technocracy was locked out. In Wilson's study he reigned, magician-king, fierce enemy to the machine age. An inhabitant of Cape Cod, reared in New Jersey, rooted in Talcottville, New York, Wilson was an unclassifiable type: a northern agrarian. And his bookshelves were a bulwark defying the ugly giant spawned by the Industrial Revolution.

By this time I had grown accustomed to his impatient bark, his explosive laughter, as well as to his long silences. I discovered in the formidable intellectual a core of childlike wonder. All his life Wilson had been an amateur magician, delighting in the staging of magic and puppet shows for the young, and I suspected that at those times he was both the performer and the beholder. Also, the clear-headed eighteenth-century rationalist was often tempted into foggier regions. Wilson went on with his study of religious metaphysics, the seductive snake in the garden of pure reason. He would splutter and inveigh against "ignorant superstitions" and the evils of the Catholic Church, but his shelves were filled with many well-thumbed tomes on religions of all times from every part of the world.

The storm continued and we were contented in the library. It was an enclosed room, almost windowless, yet the books were openings leading everywhere. And Wilson was an ideal guide, at once pedagogue and scholar. At this period he was rereading Dickens, for him a much-repeated occupation. On the morning of his death a dog-eared copy of *The Mystery of Edwin Drood* was found by his bedside. My experience with Dickens consisted mainly of childhood acquaintance with *David Copperfield* and *Oliver Twist* and later reading out loud to my young restless son, enveloped in steam from the croup kettle and accompanied by its medicinal gurgle. I was ignorant enough to say to Edmund Wilson that Dickens was not to my taste. An explosion followed. Wilson remained seated, but he looked as though he were in the thick of battle. He did not raise his voice, but it became a rocket directed at the density of my ignorance. "Have you ever read *Little Dorrit?*" he stammered. "No—well go home and do it!" His violence was ignition as was the discourse that followed. That winter I wallowed in Dickens. In a belated awakening I read all of it and nothing else. But I was constantly mindful, too, of Wilson in his library on a snowy afternoon. I recalled the Hebrew saying near his desk, the stuffed owl and the multitude of volumes opening out upon discovery.

As he grew old, irascible and ill, his appearances in the other rooms became rarer and more brief. In his study he would examine a picture book of grotesque statuary, a garden of perverted shapes outside a Renaissance Italian palace. The Beasts of Bomarzo were favorites of his, representing the utmost audacity of the twisted imagination. Once he looked up and remarked wistfully, "I never saw all of it. The steps were too much for me." But the opened book was restorative. Wilson was approaching eighty: more bald—at times fatter, at other times, alarmingly shrunken, his steps tottering, a glass of whiskey, an indispensable crutch. A prisoner in the house, he could no longer travel; even walks on the beach had become too strenuous, and he was dependent on the gentle routine of afternoon drives, with Elena as chauffeur. Yet at moments in the library, through a prestidigitator's trick, like a scarlet kerchief conjured out of a black top hat, Edmund Wilson in his prime would reemerge before our astonished eyes.

After his death every room in the house in Wellfleet withered: The blue room, so much Elena's, suffered from the disappearance of its important visitor, the imperious Old King Cole. In the kitchen, with a lightened workload, Elena appeared more tired, vaguer than before, and the ashtrays were filled to overflowing. The formal sitting room, Mary McCarthy's domain, looked like a funeral parlor, the dining room was as closed as a summer hotel at season's end and the stacks of books in the bedrooms looked dull with disuse. My husband and I felt ill at ease in the spaciousness of Edmund's wing: our privileged intimacy with the library was wasted and we shared the wish to flee from the deserted house.

Elena, always at home in the outdoors, led me to an unfrequented beach discovered by her and Brown on their off-season rambles. Here we were unaware of the vacationers nearby, packed like sardines on other sands accompanied by their transistors and their picnic hampers of martinis and the areas for nude bathers that had grown into a focal attraction for tourist curiosity, like a zoo or a freak show. Brown trotted briskly, with a proprietary air, at the water's edge. The harsh cries of gulls interrupted the monotonous crash of the waves, and our prone bodies were dots punctuating the grandeur of solitude. Soothed, we sensed that the implacability of nature was an antidote to the implacability of death. Elena reveled like a dolphin in the buffeting, rolling waves. Then, saturated by salt, encrusted with sand, we made our way through the woods to a secret pond, tepid and dark green from the reflection of leaves and its mud bottom. It was an "aftercure" following the ocean's rough massage. We bathed languidly in the freshwater basin. I watched Elena surfacing: only her face emerged. With her hair slicked severely back I was astonished by her beauty: her eyes intensely blue against the tan of her skin, the cheekbones, the sensitive nose, the puckered mouth were familiar. Yet she looked different, as though I were seeing her for the first time, as strange as a dryad. "You look like Greta Garbo!" I exclaimed. She scowled. I had displeased her in some way. "Oh, all that is finished," she said. At that moment I understood that despite her sad role of widow and the mounting years, Elena was still growing. For her, experience was like a stone dropped into the depths of a pond, causing widening circles to appear on its serene surface. She was reluctant to look back and she associated her beauty with the past. She did not realize that this was a new beauty, very much part of today. But I took comfort in the thought that growing old does not of necessity mean diminishment. I watched Elena swimming with sure graceful strokes toward the far shore, surrounded by the quiet dignity of the wooded scene at the close of day.

A year has passed since our last visit to Wellfleet, but the house is firmly reestablished in recollection as though it had been materially repaired and endowed with new vigor. Even Mary McCarthy's waxwork parlor has been converted into an office for Elena, and Edmund's library, in the hands of assessors in preparation for sale, has, nevertheless, been restored in memory to its original state. At Thanksgiving time, my husband and I settled once more into the Wilson wing. We agreed with Elena that this section of the house should not be relegated to a shrine, but we felt like visitors to a famous grave. The Hebrew inscription enduring in place near Edmund's desk had lost its meaning. It had become an archaic scrawl proclaiming the futility of human effort rather than its glory.

But something new had been added to the library. On an open drop-leaf table a series of paper folders were arranged in neat rows. White and rectangular, they resembled tombstones in a well-kept cemetery. They were labeled: "1912," "The '20s," "The '30s," "The '40s," "The '50s," "The '60s," and "The '70s"—the letters of Edmund Wilson that Elena had been gathering and editing during many months in preparation for publication.

That day we did not go outside. The dunes etched

sharply against the November sunshine were abandoned by us. We remained in the library reading: letters conjuring up Wilson's childhood already dedicated to a precocious passion for books, Princeton days, followed by World War I, then Greenwich Village and its vanished tribe of devotees led by the flaming Edna St. Vincent Millay, the thirties—Depression years—the rise and fall of the Soviet ideal, old friends, their deaths, joys, grief, and the solace of work—literature, politics, art in review, travel, a cast of characters picked from the staff and writers of *The New Republic, Vanity Fair,* and later *The New Yorker*, World War II, Europe binding its wounds, the Joseph McCarthy era, the fifties and sixties—recently fled—already history, the seventies and Edmund's last days; his increasing prickly isolation and his love for the land where were his roots. We read on greedily, the vista spread before us like a film in which we lost ourselves. But I found Edmund Wilson more clearly outlined than when he had been living: the abrasive, dedicated, honest, cranky, brilliant individualist. He loomed behind the events and the people analyzed and described in his correspondence. There he was, exploding with enthusiasm or disdain, rotund and owl-like with his claret-color, hooded eyes. The paper folders were not a graveyard. Rather they were steps toward a kind of resurrection suited to that bookish wizard, the presiding genius of the study-fortress. Edmund Wilson and his library were alive again.

We read through most of the night. And when we gathered in the kitchen at breakfast time no one was tired. We were exhilarated, a victorious army of three that had been present at the routing of death and passing time. Elena was puttering absent-mindedly between stove and table. Her worn slacks and sweater had elegance, her wavy blond hair was fairer because of the gray and she was glowing as though just off the ski slopes of an Alpine resort in the days of her youth.

Chapter Three

THE ROAD TO MANDALAY

At first glance the picture on the card appeared to be Cape Cod. This was to be expected, because it was summer, when my post office box often contains greetings from some beach where refugees from the city stretched out in the sun, oiled and relaxed, are overtaken by a day of rain, confined to a sandy cottage, and reduced to writing friends back home. On second glance, the jut of land into the blatant blue water looked foreign. I turned the card over and read: "Tomorrow Peking!" The signature: "Dinah and Jimmy." I noted the Hong Kong stamp and I understood that the Sheeans, so many years later, were once more on the road to where the action was most intense, having fled their retreat on a lake in northern Italy.

Sometimes people can be recalled most clearly after they have been removed by death or geographical distance. Some insignificant object, sight, sound, or smell is empowered to return them more vividly than those we encounter each day. The Sheeans have become part of this company. Their paths no longer cross mine. During many years we met by accident or by design, and yet, although they were certainly a most dramatic, handsome couple, for some reason the early days of our acquaintance made little impression on me. During World War II they were correspondents in the old-fashioned romantic style. Together they covered the Spanish Civil War, burning for a cause, charging their courage to the very limits of their personal strength. James Vincent Sheean had been everywhere: recording the London blitz, the Italian, French, North African theaters of war, the Pacific. Before our meeting, his best-selling memoir, *Personal History*, his view of the already legendary early days of Communism in China and Russia in the 1920s and 30s, had been published.

My initial introduction to the Sheeans has been mislaid in a haze of forgetfulness. I do remember one scene from that period because of its oddness. It is like a dream recalled in minute detail, and like a dream it is apparently senseless. The setting is my mother-in-law's town house, the time is mid-morning soon after the end of World War II. I see a gathering in the stately drawing room which is complete with conservatory, velvet upholstery, and damask drapes. But the actors appear to be featureless; only the Sheeans, the leads, are rescued from this erasure. He is tall, with a fair boyish face although he is already in his forties. She, some fifteen years younger (my age), a beauty, has long wild black hair, clear blue eyes, and high color. She reminds me of a heroine from an English novel, an apparition blown into the house on East Ninety-third Street from some windy moor. But, strangely, she is wearing a loose floor-length velvet gown that looks as though it had been retrieved from the wardrobe trunk of her famous Shakespearean actor parents: Sir Johnston Forbes-Robertson and Gertrude Elliott. The plot of the improbable dream revolves around the fire in Dorothy Thompson's Bronxville villa where the Sheeans have been living with their two small daughters. I had seen its false Tudor complacency, so unsuited to this couple returned from their passionate far-flung adventures. In my mind's eye it appeared as though two flames had been trapped inside a cardboard doll's house and had demolished it in angry conflagration. All had escaped. But what were they doing here surrounded by this faceless group? And why were my husband and I included? True, Jimmy Sheean had been a longstanding friend of my mother-in-law's, and my husband and Dinah had together compiled a book of war letters from Britain. But was this a rescue committee, a social gathering, a charitable event? As in a dream the scene persists in meaning-lessness. Only the details are telling, and Dinah's crumpled emerald-green velvet robe worn at mid-morning appears, in retrospect, like a flag signaling sudden danger and disaster. The play is without beginning or end and I did not see the Sheeans again for a long time, nor do I remember giving any thought to them during those years.

The next appearance of Vincent Sheean causes me to wonder at my blindness. One's attention is like a lighthouse illuminated by the imagination, which revolves to reveal a section of landscape here, a figure there, leaving all else in comparative darkness. It was at Marlboro College, at a writers' conference, that Vincent Sheean appeared again.

At that time he was living in nearby Vermont, alone, as he and Dinah had been divorced. He was guest speaker at the symposium and I recall his entrance into the auditorium out of a dark sultry rainy night. He looked the perfect prototype of foreign correspondent in a dripping trench coat, collar turned up, belted, with something swashbuckling and romantic about his appearance—but solitary, as though the many sights he had seen, the miles he had traveled had been seen and traveled alone. I remember nothing of his lecture, and although my husband and I talked with him afterwards, no word of the conversation is recorded in my memory. But I did observe that his face had remained boyish, though his fair hair was turning gray and receding to reveal the high-domed forehead of a prophet. His small blue eyes were penetrating but looked pained, and he squinted as though he were staring into a hurtful sun.

Why was I so neglectful of him that evening when later he was to be of so much interest? These selections, seemingly so capricious and mysterious, are, I suppose, based on subconscious needs that alter and disappear.

There was another lapse of years and Dinah Sheean telephoned to invite us for dinner. She and Jimmy had been remarried but were living separately in New York apartments. Hers, in the Murray Hill area, was cluttered with murky Victorian portraits, memorabilia of her famous actor parents and their cohorts, and stacks of books, papers, a typewriter—evidence of her own work. The room had a slovenly aspect like a bohemian eccentric. Dinah was more at home on the road than contained in a mold of domesticity. But her enthusiasm and responsiveness provided a hearth. She was still handsome, but the long free black hair had been tamed into a cropped head of crisp graying curls, and she had grown heavier. Her clear blue eyes and high color remained unchanged as well as her beautiful contralto voice and faultless English.

"Jimmy is coming for dinner," she said as though honoring us with a deity. In spite of the ups and downs of their relationship, the separations, battles, and disappointments, she had managed to preserve some of the image of the adventurous, idealistic writer she had married, who for her would always retain a touch of genius.

When Jimmy arrived I was startled to see that he was old. The reaction was a subjective one. It is always a shock after the passage of years to realize that people are not frozen into the age when last seen but have moved inexorably along an escalator, and to realize that we are moving too. A lapse in time uncovers buried thoughts; it is the skeleton at the spectacle. Jimmy had grown portly, he had a paunch, and his nose was gross and covered with a network of red, the map of years of hard drinking. The fringe surrounding his high forehead was white, he stooped and shuffled. But his greeting had the remembered hint of midwestern twang under its layer of declamatory theatricality.

The evening proceeded in a friendly unremarkable way, interspersed with the do-you-remembers of long acquaintance-ship. As usual the dialogue has vanished; only pictures remain. For this reason, there is no logical path to my tardy discovery of Vincent Sheean, nor do I know a specific reason for it. After dinner, Dinah, my husband and I, and an anonymous couple were grouped at one side of the room and Jimmy in a rocker was opposite us. All at once, he seemed to be transformed, to tower, threatening the intimate scene. He was in profile to me: I see his domed forehead, one hand with long tapering fingers raised in prophetic gesture. Here was someone worth studying, although I sensed that for me he would always remain elusive, a puzzle. Then and there I determined to read every one of his books, to find him in them and to recover, as much as possible, lost time.

It is accurate to state that I came to know Vincent Sheean through his works and that our meetings during the years when we were neighbors in New York City did little to detract from that relationship. I began with the rereading of *Personal History*; why had I previously been untouched by the conflict between the questing idealist and the hedonist addicted to luxurious living, seduced by the spurious glitter of the very wealthy and the worldly famous? I continued with *Not Peace but a Sword* (on the Spanish Civil War) and his World War II memoirs: *Between the Thunder and the Sun* and *This House Against This House*. I devoured them without interruption. Recognition through literature may cause the heart to pound like love; it is as rare and, in its way, as mysterious, never based solely on abstract merit. Why did these books come to mean so much to me, so late, after the events described in them had passed on into history? Why had I overlooked them when they were in vogue? Some chance granted me the privilege of reading them together; the works of an author depend upon one another, enhancing each other so that even the flaws and eccentricities become attractive and we wholeheartedly assume their obsessions as our own. In his books Vincent Sheean reveals two selves equally: the poet–dreamer and the man of action, a dichotomy especially attractive to me. He possesses a lyrical identification with place and there is almost no corner of the earth that has not imprinted itself on his sensibility—and I cannot help feeling that, in return, his intense vision has left an enduring impression in its wake.

Perhaps the man of action in Sheean's war books appeals to me because my view of the war had been so sequestered, self-centered, concentrated on those close to me, while his ranged far and wide, motivated by a patriotism I have never experienced. Despite his keen intelligence he reveals himself to be more idealistic and intuitive than analytical. His words throw open a thrilling world. For this, long after the events described, I thank him. I followed these books with his biographies and memoirs of other people: his delicate, sentient portrait of Edna St. Vincent Millay, the more intimate and probing recollections of Dorothy Thompson and Sinclair Lewis, the biographies of Verdi and Gandhi—the latter somewhat superficial, not altogether successful, but disclosing the mystical side of Sheean, a kind of Irish-American guru with alternating qualities of susceptibility and detachment. His attitude to the Mahatma is filial, worshipful; he had arrived from Vermont to sit at the "Bapu's" feet for life, he believed, on the very day of the assassination. What novelist can compete with the peculiar dramatic coincidences that certain lives attract? Finally I came to the book I was to reread most frequently, *First and Last Love*, the chronicle of

Sheean's lifelong love affair with music. It began during his childhood in Pana, Illinois, grew during his college years at the University of Chicago, flourished with the rise of his career as foreign correspondent, and continued all his life. He has been ardently present at every opera house and concert hall in the world. In spite of his thorough self-taught knowledge of music, he is awed and shy in the presence of virtuosos. I have often heard him exclaim, "In my next reincarnation I want to be an opera singer!"

I am persuaded that his wish may be granted because there is an uncanny identification between him and my own joy in music, especially opera. When I listen to Verdi's *Falstaff*, Jimmy is there. The bravura, the blustery passions, the bawdy comedy, clownishness, delicate tenderness, and the melancholy of Verdi's sublime music characterizing Shakespeare's aging, fat, tipsy courtier do not so much remind me of Jimmy as return him with supernatural immediacy. Far away, mostly forgotten and unbidden, he appears more real than when we were actually sitting side by side at the dinner table long ago.

For several years he lived three blocks from us across Third Avenue. New York divides itself into numerous residential sections, small villages within its vastness. So I would frequently run into Jimmy in our neighborhood and we would hail one another with the familiarity of fellow visitors on the esplanade of some spa or seaside resort. But we were environed by jerry-built apartment buildings, cafeterias, bars, laundromats, and supermarkets. As I watched him approach he would seem out of place, the world traveler grounded here. He was a little shabby and would sometimes be wearing a blue beret reminiscent of Montparnasse or Trastevere. It looked insignificant perched at a jaunty angle atop his large Churchillian head. He used a cane with swagger and I never could decide whether it was ornament or necessity. His walk was slightly pigeon-toed, vaguely childlike. But the bulk and height of his frame were impressive—yet sad, too: He reminded me of one of those huge ocean liners docked in a Hudson pier and now used only for Caribbean cruises where once it had constituted the sole means of crossing the great Atlantic Ocean. Our greeting would be banal and we would move on in our different directions. But at odd hours, often late at night, he would call—I suspect, drunk. He used his friends to expound, on the telephone, his rage and grief at the way the world was going: the Vietnam war, the Israelis and the Arabs, the plight of the blacks—and over all, his shame and pride, his love and hatred of his own country and his identification with its guilt.

It was difficult to lure him to our house, out of his lair. I had never been inside but I pictured it crammed with books and his beloved records and he had told me that it overlooked Manhattan House. I imagine that this view into the abodes of the very rich was not displeasing to him! It is my belief that at this period the crossing of Third Avenue was more of an enterprise for Jimmy than his occasional trips to Saudi Arabia to visit King Faisal in connection with a book he was then working on. Space, like time, is comparative, subject to state of mind, and in certain moods three city blocks can stretch as wide as the world.

When he did arrive for dinner he was often high, uproarious, outrageous, with that brand of humor that is the other side of sadness. I recall one evening in particular when he and Joe Liebling composed ad lib dirty limericks on (of all subjects) Willa Cather while Jean Stafford, Liebling's wife, and my husband and I implored them to stop to allow us to regain our breath and ease our aching ribs. But they went on, irrepressible, inexhaustible, and the limericks proliferated into the small hours of the morning. At other times, Jimmy, always a profuse name-dropper, would compose cables of warning, congratulations, condolence, advice, or salutation to such varied characters as Winston Churchill, Nehru, Eleanor Roosevelt, Martin Luther King, Lady Diana Duff-Cooper, Golda Meir, or Leontyne Price.

Once or twice during the summer my husband and I would coax him out of his hibernation for a weekend at our house. But it was never a success. I do not believe that suburban family life had ever been a congenial environment for Jimmy, and after we returned him in front of his apartment canopy I saw him disappear inside the welcoming obscurity of his own lobby like a great bear released from behind the bars of a zoo into his native forest.

The elegance of formal dinner parties was more attractive to him. He was able to kindle to evening attire, jewels, expensive wine. When I went with him to the new opera house at Lincoln Center we would dress with the pomp of visiting royalty, although, much to his disgust, we might be surrounded by blue jeans and matted, lank, androgynous locks. But *Die Walküre*, *Tosca*, or *La Traviata* were cure-alls. They formed an enduring bridge spanning past and present, a recourse when all else failed.

After reading Henri Troyat's biography of Leo Tolstoy, I devoted a winter to the reading and rereading of that writer exclusively, in much the same way as I had immersed myself in the books of Vincent Sheean. To crown my Tolstoy season Jimmy decided that I must visit his old friend Alexandra Tolstaya (youngest daughter of the author), at the émigré commune she founded at Blauveldt on the Hudson.

The time came in early March, a Sunday: Jimmy warned us that we would have to attend the Orthodox service at the community church and that we would be obliged, according to custom, to remain standing throughout the long ceremony. It was a muggy day and the air was as oppressive as a saturated blanket. It was too soon for signs of spring, and as the four of us—my husband and I, Jimmy and Dinah—moved along the parkway, the country drained of all color. There was no hint or promise of the season to come. Barren trees, earth, sky were etched in gray, brown, and black, submissive to the steady downpour. As my husband drove, the windshield wipers hummed and we were rather silent, even Jimmy, as though we were conserving our energy for the strain of the service we were about to attend.

The church was small, onion-domed, oddly alien set down on New York State farmland. Within, it was dark, stifling, and crowded. Through the obscurity I made out that the worshipers were all elderly or ancient, the last relics of the Czarist regime. The men—in the minority—wore frayed dark suits that had seen better days; the women were shrouded in drab shawls and looked like old-time immigrants huddled at Ellis Island. The ritual was endless, incomprehensible to me, and after a while I felt myself swaying on my feet. My husband and Dinah looked exhausted and restless too—only Jimmy stood erect, his eyes fixed straight ahead to the altar with its icons and flickering candles.

At the close of the ceremony the old people filed outside in a slow march, huddled under dripping black umbrellas. Suddenly Jimmy, breaking rank, rushed forward and stopped before the figure of a diminutive shawled woman. Bowing low, in courtier style, he raised her shriveled hand to his lips and kissed it, murmuring reverently the name of Countess Tolstaya. I shall never forget the expression on the woman's wrinkled face: a combination of incredulity and coquetry. How long had it been since a gallant courtier had bowed over her hand? At that moment no plumed hat, satin breeches, or decorations could have rendered Jimmy more aristocratic, and the drab woolen shawl might have been part of a sweeping court ball gown. But the error was soon revealed: It was not Alexandra Tolstaya, but an anonymous member of her flock. Jimmy blushed when he discovered his mistake but it was evident that he had given to the homesick transplanted little old woman a moment of intense unexpected joy—a whiff of olden days lost in the new country, a brief return of her own vanished prestige. It was explained that Countess Tolstaya had not attended the service and that we would find her at her cottage where she was awaiting us.

When we were ushered into her presence I experienced a shock. Here, lacking only the flowing beard, was the old Tolstoy himself. The resemblance between father and daughter was uncanny. She was a hulking woman in her eighties but strong and vigorous, with her father's small intelligent eyes, his wide turnip nose, and his imposing head which had something Jovian about its proportions.

Jimmy, recovered from his mistake, was soon at ease with his "old friend." We had a plentiful but coarse lunch with Countess Tolstaya in the common dining hall, while she explained the operation of the commune, its self-sufficiency, and its perpetuation. When I took stock of the average age, the latter seemed dubious. It would not be long before they would all vanish beneath the ground of the cemetery in the lee of the small onion-domed church. Alexandra Tolstaya herself was an anachronism, although a flourishing one who looked as though she might live forever. She ate like a *mujik* and was violent in her denunciation of Communists. Her attitude indicated that it would not surprise her to find one lurking beneath each dining hall table. And her forceful muscular person convinced me that she would be able to roll up her sleeves and deal effectively by herself with each enemy. Jimmy mentioned my reading of the Troyat biography. "Ugh! a disgusting book! It should never have been allowed publication. What an ugly, lying portrait of my father!" she replied. Although I did not agree with her I could understand her recoil. The intimate diaries of her parents, exhibited for all the world to see, were a public undressing, and I was aware that my interest in the book was in part a kind of keyhole peeping at the great. It was obvious that to Alexandra Tolystaya, still her father's ardent disciple, he had been defamed. Strangers should know him through his work alone.

Returned to her living quarters, we were introduced to her partner. She was younger than Countess Tolstaya and it was obvious that their relationship was scratchy and competitive. She looked like any headmistress of a boarding school. It was explained that she had not joined us at lunch as she was recovering from the flu. The conversation grew dull and I amused myself by examining the collection of old family photographs that had been smuggled out of Russia. The pictures of Tolstoy's wife and sister as young women attracted me in particular. Both were brunette, pretty, and pert (so different from the masculine ponderous daughter of Tolstoy), and I knew that the blending of those two had produced the character of Natasha in *War and Peace*. As my attention returned to the conversation around me, my husband was asking Alexandra Tolystaya how she felt about accepting the donation of money recently received from Stalin's daughter, Svetlana. Countess Tolystaya was silent for a moment. Her small gray eyes were thoughtful, then twinkled as she answered with a shrug and a sign of pious resignation, "It was God's will!" For me the day was made. The expression in those feyes, that response! I had not only met the daughter—here was Tolstoy himself come to life again. For this opportunity I felt an impulse of gratitude to Jimmy.

Later Countess Tolstaya conducted us over the muddy saturated ground of her vegetable garden. She tended it herself and I could picture her digging and hoeing. I examined her strong, callused, gnarled hands and felt certain that the produce she cultivated must be as hardy and perennial as she was herself. In parting she presented my husband with some of her tomato seeds in a small paper packet which she skillfully folded. They flourish in our garden today—large bursting red vegetable flesh— they connect our place, like widely separated kin, with Yasnaya Polyana.

Jimmy's disgust with the United States grew in proportion to his age and the slowing down of his writing activities. He continued to pay periodic visits to King Faisal and I'm certain that royal hospitality extended from any quarter of the globe could still be pleasing to him. But he talked more and more about leaving his country forever. "I plan to die in Rome," he would say. I could not help feeling that there was something operatic in his choice—a final *addio* from the Eternal City. In spite of his sixty-odd years and poor health it was easier to believe in his living than in his dying. His obsession with his demise was like an assurance, a knocking on wood, and his boisterous gallows humor, never far from an awareness of the fleeting human condition, showed a respectful attitude to the enemy's strength. It was a defense. While others, busy and unheeding, would be suddenly felled, Jimmy would survive. So I believed, and also so wished.

True to his plan, in preparation, he moved to Rome. His

tall Churchillian presence was seen no more on Third Avenue. On an autumn visit to Rome my husband and I telephoned him at the *pensione* where he was staying. His familiar voice, midwestern, slightly theatrical, spanned the months since we had met.

My husband and I strolled toward the Borghese Gardens on the way to Jimmy's *pensione*. The street was crowded, lined on both sides by little café tables and chairs set out in the sunshine. The mob was as dense as at a carnival. Pimps, prostitutes, the over-rich, the over-poor, jostled one another, staring and commenting like the audience at a freak show. But who was audience and who was freak? It was impossible to say. Straight ahead the dark gray ancient Aurelian Wall bordering the park seemed to be surveying the jostling hordes with the composure and serenity of a sage comparing the absurdity of frail humanity with the solidity and endurance of stone. The Park was as lush as midsummer, dark green, with venerable trees providing shade like cool water. Surrounding the Villa Borghese there was a clearing of gravel paths and formal gardens, planted with zinnias and chrysanthemums. They drooped and looked dusty like a straggling remnant of the retinue that had once guarded the palace of the proud princes of the Renaissance, now thrown open to the public as a museum.

Jimmy's dwelling, *Pensione Villa Borghese*, was located outside the Gardens opposite the palace. It was shabby and inconspicuous and we were ushered into the salon, a small underfurnished room that reminded me of the visitors' parlor of a school. The ill-assorted chairs were uncomfortable, there was a rickety television set, and on the coffee table a vase of wilting pink carnations attempted in vain to add a touch of cheer. The landlady left to announce our presence, and Jimmy soon arrived in crumpled army khakis. He looked as though we had roused him from a nap. Although he appeared cheerful, a little jaunty, his mood failed. His cheer was as unavailing as the pink carnations on the coffee table that separated us. We talked of home, of the bad state of things, of mutual friends, but I had no impression of his life in Rome, except for his saying, "Every afternoon I visit the Princess Paulina across the street at the Villa Borghese." When we rose to leave, Jimmy in his creased army attire became as ceremonious as an emperor. Every farewell was, after all, perhaps the final one.

Walking back to our hotel I felt oppressed. While my husband went on I decided to visit the Borghese Palace. It was cool and dark inside with a musty smell common to all museums. I inquired of a guard the direction to Canova's famous statue of Napoleon's sister, Paulina. I found her stretched out on her marble couch, her white marble draperies falling away to disclose the perfection of her white marble body, seductive but cold. One white marble tendril escaped coyly from her white marble coiffure. So this was Jimmy's royal friend, companion to lonely ex-patriotism. Suddenly the room had the clamminess of death and the body stretched on the couch became a corpse. I hurried away into the warm sunshine, propelled by a wave of overwhelming homesickness.

Jimmy did not remain in Rome. The site chosen for his demise was discarded after all. He made several sorties back to New York City but they were, apparently, failures too. On his last visit he stayed at Dinah's empty apartment. She was in Paris accompanied by Charlie, her fiercely loyal black cocker spaniel. He was always near her like a small black shadow. She was deep in endless research for a biography of a forgotten French hero of the Revolution who had died young in Napoleon's army. Jimmy commented on this project, "It's no book, it's a way of life!" I had heard her speak of "Aristide" with characteristic verve and admiration. It occurred to me that her impression of the idealistic French soldier, long dead, might somewhat resemble the Vincent Sheean she had known and loved; her collaborator during the months of the Spanish Civil War, now grown as historic as the French Revolution.

Several years ago, in late spring Jimmy finally left the United States to live abroad. We said goodbye in a city restaurant, my husband and I not wanting to subject him again to the hostility of the trees at our country place. We waited at the bar long past the appointed hour and were about ready to give up and go home when he appeared, huge and wavering, already monstrously drunk. We squeezed ourselves around a table in the crowded room, my husband and I on the banquette against the wall, Jimmy opposite us. He was very red in the face and his eyes squinted in that pained way as though the dark restaurant reflected a hurtful sun. He drank copiously and continuously, eating nothing, toying with the expensive food on his overfilled plate. His dialogue ranged widely, incoherently, the flashes of his keen intellect and humor almost, but not completely, obliterated by alcohol. Periodically, there would be a significant silence after which he would roar, "Tell me, do you think I should marry Indira Gandhi?" The reiterated question became a leitmotif, involuntarily shared by our fellow diners. I wished the long dinner would end but kept wondering how we would ever achieve our exit with Jimmy. Once he leaned toward us across the table and stated firmly and clearly, with sudden sobriety, "It's strange, I had been looking forward to this evening and it has turned out to be nothing at all." He had uttered my unspoken thought with uncanny precision. We finally managed to maneuver him out, dropped him at Dinah's door, and drove back to the country.

I have not seen him since. He settled on Lago Maggiore, a final retreat, protected by distant snow-capped Alps, a more impregnable terrain than Third Avenue or the Borghese Gardens. And Dinah joined him there; they were reunited once again, this time, I believe, for good. Dinah is a miraculous letter writer, and wherever she happens to be she can make place and people spring to life. So I can see the apartment over a grocery store where they live with Bill, a pug, the successor to Charlie. She never complains, but I sense her confinement in their small roost. She writes buoyantly that now that Jimmy has achieved the seventies, having outlived and defeated the changeling sixties, he has become a Grand Old Man. She is stubborn in her faith that his best book is still to come. She writes about their trips to Milan to La Scala and his renewal in opera which she shares. But I have my own picture of him. It is evening and he is on his way to what he calls "his lake," revived by a visit to the local pub. He walks in that slightly pigeon-toed childish fashion and he is wearing the old blue beret. He sits on a bench under the stars gazing across the still water and talks, talks endlessly to his captive audience, the village mayor. He discourses in fluent Italian, but sometimes interjects phrases in English, French, or German like trophies from his years of travel. He quotes Shakespeare, Dante, Croce, switching effortlessly from philosophy to politics, to literature, to music. His uproarious gallows humor and his mysterious insight are like flares illuminating the stagnant lake. Night after night the mayor listens submissively, marveling at the crazy American *signor*. Now and then Jimmy pays a visit to the town post office and sends off one of his bombastic cables to President Nixon, Indira Gandhi, or Golda Meir.

I had thought that this was the closing chapter of

Jimmy's life until I received the card with its short rousing message: "Tomorrow Peking!" It was like a battle cry holding Time and its destructive army at bay. Here was no dwindling off into the wavering traceries of old age—instead, a bold line was curling around to form a complete circle.

Chapter Four

A CHUCKLE FROM THE GRAVE

Jean Stafford is dead. This morning as I was looking for a number in my address book it opened by mistake at S. I read, *Jean Stafford—Fireplace Road—Springs, Long Island*—tel: 516-324-2625.

How pitifully few and random are the memories that can be summoned at will. In reverse proportion, the closer the consanguinity, the deeper the passion, warmer the affection, the more binding the tie and the longer its duration, the more meager the collection will be. We are obliged to remember the dead in disconnected tableaux set into utter darkness.

I met Jean Stafford around nineteen-fifty, I believe in a New York apartment in a renovated brownstone in the east seventies. Although it had an air of gentility it was in the neighborhood of shabby rooming houses, some of them vacant, awaiting the arrival of the demolition crews. At that date, due to the success of her first novel, *Boston Adventure*, Jean was already known. Divorced from Robert Lowell, she had left Boston and their home in Maine and had moved, alone, to New York. I see a pretty young woman with a long wheat blond pageboy bob and pert kitten features. Although the occasion was probably a cocktail party and my husband and I brought there by some mutual friend, the others have been blotted out. A window emerges, festooned with hanging potted plants. It framed the drab side street and the silhouette of Jean Stafford who appears to be companioned, exclusively, by her two skinny, clever Siamese cats . . .

She reappears next, in memory, at our Westchester home, married now to Oliver Jensen. They were living in suburban Connecticut which she scorned, describing the local "station wagon set" in withering terms. She and Jensen were like a couple cast in a performance of *Who's Afraid of Virginia Woolf?* for summer stock. The play was to have a short run.

Her marriage to A. J. Liebling I recall, chiefly, for its groaning board spread at their apartment on lower Fifth Avenue near Washington Square. The buffet was as abundant as an overflowing cornucopia, the liquor without limit, and our barrel-shaped host and the hostess were drunk as lords.

At a gathering of academics in a university town, Jean, the writer in residence, was stretched out on a couch. At this period, she had begun to resemble a small-town librarian, prim and vaguely spinsterish. But now she was clad in a black leather jumpsuit that left her still girlish shoulders and back naked, in startling contrast to the hairy tweeds and "little" covered up cocktail dresses surrounding her. Her costume seemed to be making a statement; it looked less seductive than lonely. In any group Jean would remain stubbornly odd man out.

After the death of Joe Liebling she left the city to take up permanent residence in their Springs, East Hampton, Long Island, home. We did not meet often and her visits to New York were occasioned, mainly, by ill health. The hospital was to become her familiar *pied á terre*. Our friendship was carried on via the telephone. It was characterized, also, by her impulsive, idiosyncratic gifts. I treasure a straw cowboy's hat banded by a red kerchief and a green marble Easter egg filled with homemade potpourri.

After dialing East Hampton, there would be a recorded response: "We are at work at present. We will return your call as soon as possible. When you hear the beep", etc.—royalty addressing her subject, a teacher coolly reprimanding an insubordinate first grader. But more often than not, Jean's live voice would intercept the mechanical one and, as though we had never left off, we were launched into another interminable conversation. She spoke with slow deliberateness, her English impeccable as a philologist's, her laughter, rich and boozy, was often interrupted by bouts of helpless coughing. But she could curse like a stevedore and her discourse was laced with anachronistic colloquialisms retained from her childhood in a small Colorado mountain town.

"I haven't seen you in a month of Sundays," she might say.

Soon we were engaged in the pleasurable destruction of our enemies, but her humor could transform the field of battle into a "human comedy" of her own creation. She would save her most lethal barbs for modern writers whose abuse of English caused her to become "cross as a bear!" And she detested modishness everywhere: In recent years she threw all mail addressed to her with *Ms* into the scrap basket, unopened. Tacked on her back door, outside the spic-and-span kitchen, there was a no-welcome sign embellished with hand-drawn rosettes and arabesques: *The word "hopefully" must not be misused on these premises. Violators will be humiliated.*

Sometimes she would call me late at night. After an hour or so of gossip and book talk (Henry James and Mark Twain were dearest to her heart, but if a contemporary struck her fancy her championship would be fierce and independent), I might point out the hour. But she was not easily deterred. I pictured her alone with her cat in the gray-shingle salt-box house filled with its orderly, well-tended clutter of Victorian furniture and bric-a-brac—upstairs and down a profusion of desks, serious ones equipped with typewriters, as well as impractical antiques. A dainty specimen, resembling a spinet, graced an alcove. When I asked about its function, she had replied with one of her wheezing chuckles,

"Oh that—it's for condolence notes."

Her bedroom was chaste, white, her bed good early American but near it, in case of an emergency brought on by emphysema, stood a group of tall green oxygen cylinders. They reminded me of the cypress tress that grow in a pastoral cemetery. I believe that her house was too far away for her to hear the waves from the bedroom window. But during our nocturnal conversations I fancied that the orchestra of Westchester crickets I listened to had its counterpart on the dunes and in the potato fields of the Hamptons. When thunder threatened our dialogue and the wires crackled dangerously, she would say, referring to the storm,

"It's a lulu!"

"Jean, I think we had better stop."

"I'll hang up p.d.q."

But she never did. It took a long time to dispose of the final victim, pickled in her special flavorsome recipe of brine.

For me, in winter, our telephone visits were accompanied by sociable city noises: the traction of tires on snowy streets, the steady hum of traffic, a disembodied voice beneath my window calling a cheerful goodnight to an unseen companion. I knew Jean's isolation. The brave shingle salt-box house rode the silent white fields, alone. Within, its mistress cuddled, hedged among the quaint furniture and bric-a-brac. Perhaps, Elephi the cat was curled up beside her on the bed. During the Christmas season Jean used to complain about her work on an annual round-up of children's books for *The New Yorker*. A female Scrooge, she would sneer,

"Gosh darned sanitized pap! Give me the bad witches and demons, the scalding cauldrons and evil spells of the old days!"

And as in olden times, I saw her house hung with bushy, country holly wreaths, the hearth in flame, the mulled wine she served her neighbors (those she was not feuding with on that particular holiday) was strong, aromatic with cloves and sticks of cinnamon.

The last times I saw Jean, shortly before her death, have receded and seem as distant as our initial meeting. The pretty young woman with the kitten's face had been turned into a skeleton, the pert features sunk into a living skull. She had suffered a stroke and the most articulate person I have ever known was able to utter, after strenuous struggle, only single, strangled, hard-won words, between painful, choked silences. The elegant writer no longer composed her witty, touching stories and novels, her shapely essays. The typewriters were unemployed and she was just able laboriously to sign her name with the aid of a sample signature.

As my husband and I waited for her to descend from her room in a New York City club where she was staying, the grandfather's clock in the hall struck five: the stately tea hour in this old house that once had been a private mansion.

Across the threshold of the deserted library, Jean came towards us. A black silk dress with a sagging hem hung from her desiccated body. But I noticed that she was wearing coquettish, scarlet, nineteen-forties-style pumps and she carried a bag to match: the aging, ailing small-town librarian attired for a spree in the big city. We sat in front of the empty baronial stone fireplace and, in her halting fashion, she managed to communicate that she had decided to sell her house in Springs—move to New York, see old friends. My husband and I waited out the excruciating pauses. Once when a word refused to come, she buried her head, with its cropped, mahogany-dyed hair, in her claw-like hands.

"Oh, God! Oh, God!"

But looking up again she proposed with surprising sprightliness,

"Let's have a drink."

It was Saturday afternoon and, in accordance with club rules, the bar was shut.

In the lift, Jean remounted to her room. She returned clasping a bottle of whiskey; a starving mother hugging to her bosom a beloved, oversized infant. As we sat, more relaxed now, over our drinks, I noticed on a silver chain around her neck a man's old-fashioned pocket watch. Perhaps it had belonged to her father, alias Jack Wonder, a writer of Western adventure books. And, perhaps, at the close of her life, she was turning away from the sophistication of the East, back to her beginnings in the cruder, wider West. The hands on the white moon face of the watch pointed to six and the grandfather's clock in the hall chimed the same hour: sad reminders, both, of the mortal passing of time.

My final visit with Jean took place at the New York hospital where she had been taken from the club. She had ventured forth without the green oxygen cylinders and had nearly died in the intensive care ward. But she reemerged, still fighting. Although the hospital was her place of refuge, her true club, she socialized with no one there. The exception was her doctor, who,

I am certain, had to stand for a great deal of abuse. As soon as I entered her room, she jumped spryly off the bed and led me down the corridor to the stifling steam-heated lounge. From an institutional settee, she played hostess as though ensconced in her antimacassered armchair in the parlor at home. She wore a long velvet robe with the demure white ruffle of her nightgown showing beneath her chin; she looked almost pretty again. In defiance of her doctor's orders, she smoked incessantly, lighting one cigarette from another. Her words were as reluctant as ever, but they seemed charged with the old vehemence and she responded to my monologue of anecdotes with appreciative, juicy chuckles.

She died a week later in a rehabilitation institution where she had been sent by her doctor, as she refused to return home with a nurse and was too sick to live alone in New York. I hate to think of her in that barrack for the disabled, subject to its rules and regulations, urged to join group therapy and to applaud the efforts of the other inmates. Jean, the proud, the isolated, the tender misanthrope could not have endured that ugly communal existence.

"Get—me—out—of here—get—me—out—of here—" she scolded.

But no one did and her heart stopped, arrested, at last, by the inelasticity of her extinguishing lungs.

Priests, rabbis, and ministers, in addition to their metaphysical consolations, tell us that the dead survive through their good deeds on earth and in the minds and hearts of those who loved them. But I am not solaced by my album of souvenir snapshots. Can that be all the years are enabled to redeem? In the case of Jean Stafford there is something more.

Since her death I have reread her collected stories which,

at the time of their publication, won her the Pulitzer Prize. She has not ordered them chronologically; they are grouped, instead, under regional titles: *Innocents Abroad, The Bostonians and Other Manifestations, Cowboys, Indians and Magic Mountains, Manhattan Island*. This, in itself, tells us a great deal about Jean Stafford. Like her idol, Henry James, she was a "homesick" writer, one of the breed who, while nourished by their roots, are driven by unappeased curiosity, rebellion, and a longing for new places and different people. Good literature does not grow in the soil of a peaceful mind, nor unquestioning spirit. As James was a self-styled Londoner, Jean was converted to New England. But she often looked back with a cool, humorous, unsentimental regard to the Colorado of her growing up. Although she had a hearty appetite for the "adventures" met in Boston, Manhattan, and abroad, they could precipitate attacks of mental indigestion: disappointment permeates her stories. Yet the disillusion is mediated by her unfailing wit and an undramatized stoicism inherited from her pioneering forebears. She could not resist the lure of Pinckney Street, Fifth Avenue, or the playgrounds and capitals of Europe and she was often tricked into mistaking the sham for the real. But, upon recovery, she would model a character or shape a plot from the basic, opposed materials of innocence and irony. Always, she would be drawn to the manicured gardens and interiors of inherited wealth, viewing them with the star-dusted gaze of a poet. But the same eye that constructed those "castles in the air," destroyed them. We are grateful for both the visions and the honesty that brought them down.

Jean's childhood was spent in a mountain town she calls Adams. Her mother, a practical nurse, tended the consumptives who came there to be healed by the altitude and the pure air.

Because Jean was a tough-minded author, who fended off the treacheries of the heart, the child heroines from her past are, in the main, "bad characters": fighting, scratching hellions, kleptomaniacs, gawky misfits, tomboys, and wild cats. Yet the reader loves them, while remaining cold to the meek "little women" and child wives of Victorian literature. For animals, household pets as well as the miserable caged beasts in the zoo, Jean would permit herself the indulgence of demonstrated affection. But the disciplined emotion of a large heart is all the more powerful for being dammed.

The people of her foreign tales (I include here Boston, New York City, and their environs, as Jean was a perpetual outlander) are mostly elderly. She was rarely concerned with the ages between early adolescence and old age. Notable exceptions and most successful ones are: "Children Are Bored on Sunday," "A Country Love Story," and "The Interior Castle." The first deals with a tentative attraction, a chance meeting between a lonely young woman and man lost in the vastness of New York City, the second, with the death of a marriage in a farmhouse in Maine, while the third reveals Jean's intimacy with hospital life and the lunar geography of pain. Perhaps it was her prickly, virginal quality that caused her to leap across the middle years with their sexual preoccupations and to concentrate on old age, a state she barely reached herself. But one identifies her with the octogenarians, full of grit and iron, who from wheelchair and nursing home bed, shut-ins imprisoned in mansions and seedy rooming houses, direct their poisoned shafts at those who stand upright and can still walk—though usually in the wrong direction!

The scrawny little girls with scabby knees, the cantankerous, cranky old ladies are with us. Jean Stafford lives.

In a postscript to self-portraiture, a non-literary document has been uncovered since her death. It is her last will and testament, leaving everything, house, land, money, even the management of her literary estate and the royalties therefrom, to a Springs cleaning woman. From the grave, I think I hear a wicked, juicy chuckle.

Chapter Five

MANY MANSIONS

A name through habitual use clings to a person like a barnacle to a floating log, growing as much a part of him as his features or his coloring. For this reason it bothered me that my brother and Philip Rahv bore the same first name. In life I was mostly heedless of this coincidence, but as soon as I decided to commit Philip Rahv to paper it became an obstacle. These two men, so different, yet with one name! I remembered my mother in my childhood translating our Greek names: Dorothea, "gift from God"; Philip, "lover of horses." I had been well pleased by my superior status! Now in the recall of my brother and Philip Rahv, the meaning of their name takes on new significance for my own purposes. Change one letter and, presto, "lover of horses" becomes lover of houses—the one characteristic shared by both. The performance of this small trick having established the "Philip" part of them to my satisfaction, I can proceed, confident that though names or words may be impressive in themselves they can never come close to encompassing the mystery and multiplicity of a single human equation.

I met Philip Rahv on a Saint Patrick's Day in the late 1940s at the home of Emmy and Louis Kronenberger, then theater critic for *Time* magazine. I know the date because it was the night of a record end-of-winter blizzard. Fresh snow in New York City is magic despite the subsequent filth, confusion, and paralysis it causes. Silent, it hushes the general noise, obliterates time, and alters space. It transforms the metropolis into the same small town we glimpsed in childhood, resurrected every time there is a heavy, soft, muted fall of snow. I can see the glistening crust close to my eyes as I lie face down on my belly while my father pulls my sled toward Central Park, redecorated in white on this Sunday morning to resemble an alpine resort. Or, years later it is a weekday and due to the severity of the storm all automobiles have been banned from the streets. But my husband, with the temerity of a North Pole explorer, defying nature, chooses to ignore the order. Rounding up our small son and his friends, he packs them into his car and heads for school. With his load of ski-suited, hooded, mittened, booted children eager and curious in this strange newborn world, he proceeds cautiously along the deserted streets, skidding between high white banks, the chains on his tires clanking and crunching in the unaccustomed silence. He is Admiral Byrd but he is also, partly, the homey, reassuring narrator of Thornton Wilder's play *Our Town*, and the boys and girls are the citizens of a temporary hamlet, far more exciting than the crowds and clamor of their native city. All my Christmases are joined—those of my childhood, my son's and my granddaughters'—by the presence, the anticipation, or the hope of that same snowstorm, appearing again and again to astound our vision and make us lose track of the passage of time.

Shelter is intensified when it snows and houses become unusually alluring. Perhaps this is one reason I remember that particular party we went to at the Kronenbergers'. They lived on Ninety-fifth Street between Lexington Avenue and Park. The block is unchanged; it has a small-town ambience and is lined with small private houses, their front doors painted bright red, green, or blue. Many are high-stooped, all are solid but unstylish like prosperous shopkeepers of the neighborhood, in contrast to their more socially aristocratic peers to the south. The atmosphere is old-fashioned and snug and on that Saint Patrick's eve with the snow gaining momentum outside, the Kronenbergers' house enclosed us in warmth. The narrow entrance was already filled with discarded wraps suspended from a clothes rack rented for the occasion. Beneath it were galoshes with melting snow still clinging to them and damp umbrellas huddled like chaperones on the periphery of the party already under way in the living room and the adjoining dining room, overheated, vibrating to the multivoiced roar of a literary gathering.

Many of the faces are lost to me. Perhaps this is because youth is too intent on its own image to enable it to see others clearly. At that time, on entering a crowded room, anticipation and uncertainty took possession of me and just as a traveler starting out upon a journey is caught up by the sensations of motion and change themselves and is too excited to see out of the window of the train or plane, I too was missing the fleeting scene. I do recall W. H. Auden, old even then, his face a map of lines; Lionel Trilling, writer, professor, slight and shadowy gray, with a mind as drawn to pure knowledge as a moth to the light; his wife, Diana, the critic—and our host and hostess, he, elfin, cozy, and chatty, she, diminutive, with bright black eyes. I moved among countless others making conversation, taking note of my own undeveloped skills, like a novice eager to learn the intricate steps of a gavotte.

Suddenly a presence broke through my self-absorbed blindness. He was standing at the far end of the dining room, taller and broader than everyone else. He had an oversized head with a shock of black hair, was swarthy, and had a generous nose that turned up comically at the end, making it look like an implement—a sort of shovel with which to dig up the absurdities and foibles of those around him. His lips were thick but shapely and there was something poetic about their sensuality in contrast to the rest of his plebeian appearance. He looked like a truck driver set down at a gathering of college professors. Drawn to him and forgetting my diffidence, I pushed and elbowed my way to where he stood. When I drew close I observed that his large brown eyes set in dark shadowed puffs were surprisingly gentle and thoughtful yet unflinching.

I no longer remember how we started to talk, but I was hypnotized by his speech, guttural and soft, with an accent so heavy that it was all I could do to recognize a stray word here and there. Yet it was enough to convince me of his bold intelligence and a sincerity as aggressive as his physical person. I remember his talking that night—or rather lecturing—on the subject of Thomas Mann. He would emphasize his points with wide flappings of his hands interspersed by rough absent-minded nudges. Who was this man with his thick foreign accent, discussing *The Magic Mountain* and *Dr. Faustus* with such brilliance while looking like a peasant recently converted to city life? Abruptly he broke off his monologue, which seemed more like a retort. Although I had not had the chance or the courage to utter more than a few words, his pronouncements were delivered with so much combativeness as to sound like violent rebuttals directed at an invisible, inaudible opposition. After a pause, in a different tone, caressing yet impersonal and blunt, he said, "You're quite pretty. What's your name?"

He did not tell me his, and, flattered and confused, I failed to ask him. The fierce literary lecture resumed. "Dey don't write any more—dey just talk about demselves, no sense of history, no social sense, just dere own intestines. Who cares, huh?

Who do dey tink dey are?" Followed by another vigorous jab at my ribs.

I spent the remainder of the evening with him, and when the party broke up I rejoined my husband, telling him about this strange man with his thick accent, brusque manner, and astounding knowledge of literature and history. "How did he land here?" I asked. "What sort of truck driver is he?" Amazed at my ignorance, my husband answered, "He is Philip Rahv, the co-founder and editor of *Partisan Review* and a famous critic."

Afterward I remembered my first meeting with Philip and realized how characteristic of him it had been. Always aware of his ugliness, never realizing its fascination, he was nonetheless a lusty woman-taster. Yet he refused to trade on his position.

At the front door, on our way out, we met again. Now he was with his wife, Nathalie, stout, florid, and thoroughly drunk at this moment, but with a dignity that was impressive. She looked like an American Valkyrie dimmed by approaching middle age and a certain weariness. Philip bundled his bulk into an ulster, wound a thick woolen scarf around his neck, and placed an absurdly small felt hat at a rakish angle on his large head. It looked like the lid of a kitchen pot on top of a barrel. Through the open door we confronted the cold night.

The street lamps revealed the snow, unmarred by any footprints. The level had risen rapidly while we had been inside, covering the stoops and reaching up to basement windows like a minor mountain range. Snow was still falling in large crowding flakes. Now East Ninety-fifth Street looked like Moscow, but with Philip Rahv in our midst it was not the city of name-day receptions and balls but a place of intellectual and social upheaval on the eve of revolution. Far away I heard an automobile coughing its way to life out of the freeze. I was back in New York and the year was 1947. We proceeded slowly down the steep buried stoop, clinging to the wet balustrade for support. Only Nathalie in her state of aloof, regal drunkenness ignored it, and, missing the first step, down she floated. Light and buoyant as a balloon despite her heft she landed miraculously upright on her feet on the sidewalk, her immense dignity still intact. This first fantastic presentation of her remains: a lady, indestructible, proud, self-sufficient, uncommunicative and, perhaps, lonely.

After the evening at the Kronenbergers' I recall our first party at Philip and Nathalie's Greenwich Village apartment—one floor-through of an old house. The gathering had its historic aspects: It was an event that would be discussed over and over by the small group of intellectuals over which Philip presided. It was fuel for the kind of gossip that he himself relished when it was about others—but now he was center stage along with Mary McCarthy. It was a first meeting, a reconciliation after the breakup of their early love affair, and the publication of her satiric novel on academic life, *The Oasis*, in which Philip made an unpleasant appearance. An early contributor to *Partisan Review*, she had been Philip's special protégée. Now he eyed her with distrust and defiance, tinged, I thought, with a look of soft melancholy. The wounds he had suffered through her might be denied by the gruff aggression of his words but they were indelibly inscribed in his eyes. He was like a poet turned diplomat who furtively indulges his muse only after working hours, in the belief that he is unobserved. For those who knew him well, Philip was a romantic despite his self-taught hardheadedness.

He was holding forth on the "new criticism": "Why do dey try to turn de clock back? Freud, Marx, and Trotsky can never be forgotten. Nothing will ever be de same again." This was punctuated by the rough pokes and nudges at the person closest at hand. Philip was one of the army of disillusioned ex-communists. In the thirties he had cut his Party ties, viciously denouncing Stalin and the Soviets in his writings and in his talking. But he still clung to shreds of his abandoned faith, in the form of his own brand of Trotskyite socialism.

We sat in a circle in his sparsely furnished living room—on the floor, on cushions, stools, chairs borrowed from bedroom and kitchen. The walls were hung with crude examples of abstract expressionism by obscure artists. Philip's eyes were focused inward on cerebral matters, and it always seemed to me that he was blind to the visual world—with the great exception of women! And Nathalie was undomestic, concentrating on her own architect's career. The room grew hot, the conversation strenuous. I remember Delmore Schwartz, the unhappy neurotic poet. Dwight Macdonald was there, competing with Philip in audacious sallies, accompanied by high derisive laughter.

Nathalie sat by silent and inscrutable in the midst of her noisy guests. They reminded me of actors in an old film depicting the intellectual ferment of the early days of the student rebellion in Russia, viewed in the light of the present moment, with nostalgia, but through the revolving glasses of hindsight. When it was time to leave, my husband and I excavated our coats from the pile on the Rahvs' king-size bed, a fit battlefield for the private wars of two contending giants.

During the years I knew him, Philip moved from Greenwich Village to Riverside Drive, to the East Side near Bloomingdale's (where he liked to browse in the Gourmet Shop, always fancying himself a master chef), to a spacious studio off Central Park West. Although he remained essentially urban, a man who might have been at home at a European café surrounded by a coterie of international professors and writers, my most vivid pictures of him are set against bucolic backgrounds from which he stands out like a slow-moving hippopotamus incongruously transplanted from some faraway land into a field of American daisies, goldenrod, and clover. The first portrait shows him at Bridgewater, Connecticut. The house has disappeared from my view, accompanied by other faces. It is noon of a summer's day and he is sitting by the side of an old stone well that looks like the property of a transcendental commune in the New England of Emerson and Thoreau. Philip's dark shadow extending over the grass resembles a sundial, a reminder of a somber alien past projected onto the bright light of the present hour. He is dressed in slacks and a sport shirt as loud as his avant-garde paintings and he is gazing into the well. His expression is not to be forgotten: ruminating, far-seeing, and surprisingly vulnerable.

By this time I had learned something of his history—from others—as he was always stubbornly secretive about himself. He had been born in Russia and migrated during the pogroms to the United States when he was about twelve years old to join his older brother, a journalist in Providence, Rhode Island. For a short time he had been an American schoolboy, atypically old and serious, wearing a formal black suit that must have isolated him from his peers as much as his inquiring mind and his strange foreign accent. He came to New York, still in his teens, to be met by the Depression. It remains a mystery how he managed to move from bread lines, park benches, and lonely, hungry sessions in the New York Public Library, to be co-founder with William Phillips, of *Partisan Review* and to become a leading intellectual of the thirties. To some it may appear to be a demonstration of the functioning of our democratic system, but I believe it to be one of those rare glimpses of individual potential, a phenomenon hoped for at all times, in any nation, that relieves and redeems the drab uniformity of universal mediocrity.

Today, whenever I find myself on the porch of a country house, I am transported back to places no longer visited and to people many years ago. A white-shingled corner sheltering a hammock or wicker chair, pillars supporting a separate roof and framing a section of village street, meadow, river, lawn or beach, lazy noon heat, melting salmon-pink sunsets or darkness alive with the buzz of cicadas are pieces of one remembrance: summers past. Now from this mosaic I single out Philip and Nathalie Rahv's house in Millbrook, New York, the home, I believe, he loved best. I don't know its precise date but its style belonged to a vanished era. It was generously laid out and decorated on the outside with American gothic fretwork like the House of the Seven Gables. Philip showed us around its echoing rooms and I recognized some of the pieces of modern furniture and abstract paintings from the city apartments. They looked forlorn and lost, scattered over the expanse of bare floors and walls like immigrants stranded on a dock. But, in reverse, these greenhorns were from the New World thrown ashore to make their way on the strange continent of the past. Philip was installing changes, mainly modernizing the kitchen (for him always the heart of any house) and adding bathrooms. Bathrooms represented the acme of luxury, the badge of security, and he counted their number with pride, the left-wing scholar turned squire with the purchase of each new house.

My souvenirs of Millbrook are, in the main, summer ones, as Philip and Nathalie continued to spend their winters in New York City, she to pursue her career, he for the magazine and to attend those late nights of good talk and gossip. He would greet his friends avidly, "What's new? Have you heard any gossip?" I always did my best to supply him while he regarded me eagerly like a great beast awaiting the morsel of raw meat I was about to throw him. "I don't believe it!" he would exclaim, running his paw over his head until his black hair fell in disarray. "You must be kidding!" But his own stock of gossip was more copious and hours were spent in hearing about the marital problems of his acquaintances. The substance was usually psychological and analytical rather than vicious. It involved the plots of social or intellectual arrivistes or the sexual eccentricities of writers, many of whom had been launched from the pages of *Partisan Review*, full-grown plants sprung from seeds started in a cold frame within the nurturing atmosphere of a greenhouse. At the dinner hour the gossip would be halted temporarily while Philip performed his kitchen rites with the same didactic sureness he brought to his historical and literary opinions. Saffron rice—it's firm jaundiced grain—appeared with every dish. When I taste it now I hear again his soft guttural accents and I see him at the head of his table gobbling his food with the relish of a connoisseur too honest not to appreciate his own creations.

On the porch after dinner he would hold forth on politics or on his favorite writers: Tolstoi, Dostoevski, Henry James, or Proust, and, of course, the eternal triumvirate of Marx, Freud, and Trotsky. For contemporary authors, even those he had himself plucked from obscurity, he often showed surprising scorn: "Bah! What's so great about him? Who needs all dose *sthetl* fairy stories?" or "Do dey tink dey have invented sex? Dey make me sick." Saul Bellow was an exception; Philip's endorsement of him grew more emphatic with each book. But in those days his enthusiasm kept pace with his outrage. For all his misanthropy, Philip was a born teacher, irascible, impatient, biased. But just as fire purifies as it destroys, Philip's lectures cauterized the minds of his listeners and provoked in them a kindred spark. Sometimes at Millbrook he would pause to peer over the railing of the porch into the darkness outside and exclaim, "Woodchuck!" in a stentorian voice, "I ought to shoot. Dey are ruining my grass!" And he would make a move toward the gun leaning against the wall of the house. Happily he never used it in my presence—

perhaps it was not even loaded but just another prop to reassure himself that he was, indeed, an American landowner who had traveled a long road away from the little foreigner dressed in a black suit in the Providence schoolhouse or the hungry, lonely youth submerged among the dusty stacks of the New York Public Library.

When Philip and Nathalie were divorced, it was a shock, although their friends had been aware that the marriage had been shaky for some time. Nathalie, wealthy in her own right and generous, left Philip his beloved Millbrook house. She moved to Boston to continue her work, remaining Philip's friend to the day of his death.

For a while he divided his time between New York and Millbrook. I pictured him solitary on the porch, angrily staring down his old enemy, the woodchuck, while the uncut grass grew higher each day, or in the kitchen surrounded by all his equipment. He could count the number of unused bathrooms, his own always an auxiliary library now more crowded than ever with his reading matter. But it must have been a lonely existence, and Philip was basically a city man. Sadly—it was like another divorce—he sold the house. It had been an American dream that had possessed his imagination and like a dream it slipped away even while he tried to cling to it.

He accepted a professorship at Brandeis University in Waltham. And now in middle age, before it was too late, he went in search of adventure, which for him always meant another woman. He had his teeth capped and, until I grew accustomed to them, they shone out of his swarthy face as brightly as the porcelain fixtures in his bathrooms. He lost weight, bought some new clothes, and after many years revisited Europe—the Old World—again. But he soon returned to find his next wife here. After some amorous interludes it was Nathalie who introduced him to Theodora Jay Stillman. She had been a friend of Nathalie's younger sister as Nathalie had been a classmate of Mary McCarthy's at Vassar; so Philip followed a circle from one indigenous American product to the next. Theodora was descended from John Jay, Colonial statesman and jurist.

"Teo iss a lady!" he used to say, and it was true. She looked like an English noblewoman crossed by Gypsy blood in some distant past. She was as tall and massive as Nathalie but she had black hair and flashing black eyes under heavy brows. Her flesh was very white and she seemed to have more of it than most people; it covered her luxuriously like velvet. She had a straight, sharp-tipped nose with long aristocratic nostrils, inherited, perhaps, from her illustrious ancestor. Her mouth was voluptuous and she had a faint mustache. Her lips, usually half open, contradicted the firmness of her jaw and rounded chin. She dressed in bright prints: ruby, purple, emerald. But her hems sagged and the hooks were often missing or the zipper derailed at her ample waist. Philip took pleasure in decorating the white velvet expanse of her décolletage with heavy ornate antique necklaces.

Theo came to him with a house at Martha's Vineyard we had rented years before. One summer I had watched my five-year-old son gathering seashells on the beach in front of it. I remember him stooping in the unindividuated way, the immemorial pose of all children playing at the seaside. Now when I hear the shriek of gulls at once I smell wet salty air, my hair and clothes seem sticky with salt, and I can almost feel leftover sand in my shoes. When we returned fifteen years later to visit Theo and Philip the gulls were still swooping over the roof. The one that had stood sentinel on a tide-washed post in the shallow water of the bay seemed to be there still, motionless, its feathers clear gray and white, like a stuffed bird in a museum, and the sagging hammock, too, strung between two trees on the grass that sloped down to the water. In fact nothing about the house had changed; it had the same bilious sea smell, the peacock fantailed wicker chair, the papery white walls through which one heard a variety of noises: snores, coughs, protesting creaks of beds, and, outside, the ever-lasting cry of gulls.

"It's all the same! Let me look around!" I exclaimed to Philip as he put my bag down in the guest room.

"This one was ours, do you remember?" I asked my husband as we both looked out the window at the familiar view of the bay where the ferry would still ply its stolid course to the mainland. In the next room we found no disorder of gritty pails, shovels, and toy automobiles. The bathroom remained the same, commodious and old-fashioned, like a cottage living room with its chintz curtains and old rocking chair. The well-remembered tub was awkward and high as a Model-T Ford and the collection of family medicines, cosmetics, and brushes was still displayed on crude wooden shelves. In another part of the house Theo had built for Philip a more modern bathroom and had made a study out of the attic.

"Oh, it's all the same," we repeated to each other as we clattered from the back stairs to the kitchen. It was all the same, but we were different—ephemeral humans in search of our own pasts, phantoms brushing against the unyielding shell of material things.

As we sat on the porch having cocktails before lunch I observed Philip. He was dressed the same and used the same familiar gestures as when he had been our host in Millbrook. But Theo was there in place of Nathalie. With a red bandanna covering her head she appeared more Gypsy than American aristocrat. Philip was teaching her to cook without much success. Theo was willing but awkward, and occasionally crashes would issue from the kitchen as another piece of crockery was dropped and smashed to bits. Philip remained unperturbed, continuing his discourse on the downfall of the realistic novel or the dangers of a too-strong executive branch of the government. He was educating Theo outside the kitchen also. Like an enthusiastic schoolgirl she had shown me her summer reading list; I remember that it included *Jane Eyre* and *Portrait of a Lady*. One of her two daughters, "Little Theo," was there at the time. She was a teenager, extraordinarily tall and thin with long legs in tight jeans. Her beauty was wild and casual; with flowing hair and aquiline features, she looked like a youthful pirate. Philip remained aloof from his stepdaughter, but now and then he threw her a lingering, measuring sidelong glance, in the manner he reserved for all attractive females.

That other holiday with its different cast of characters was far away. There had been picnics on the beach on the surf side where the cliffs frowned over the sand and the waves reared and dashed their foaming heads on the shore. Always there were children in groups and young parents spinning out long days of laziness. A drive to some distant beach, a sail to an island in the morning and barbecues at dusk were the warp and woof of each day. After a picnic on the beach the parents would gather the debris in hampers and pick up the scattered beach toys, then everyone drugged with sun and salt water headed for home.

That evening at the Rahvs' there were guests for dinner, gathered at the candlelit refectory table: Philip Roth on the verge of his great success, *Portnoy's Complaint*; William Styron then working on *The Revolt of Nat Turner*, his wife, Rose, who looked like her name; the playwright Lillian Hellman, bitterly humorous and world-weary, yet romantic, long after, about the staunch Leftists during the vanished McCarthy era; Robert Brustein, drama critic; and a poet whose name I can no longer remember.

The conversation was spirited, contentious; still, in the wavering candlelight, I looked across at my husband—was he also searching for a group of children eating peanut butter sandwiches and for our younger selves, gone, but invoked by the well-known house existing unchanged into another age? Where are those years? What were they? I wanted to cry out to my husband. They were made up of so many things that we took for granted. Let me not take anything for granted anymore. Let the present be meaningful; let it explode so loudly that it drowns out all aching echoes of the past. But this moment too slipped by, and we all rose from the table and moved to the verandah.

"What an extraordinary stole," Rose Styron remarked to Lillian Hellman.

"Dash [Dashiell Hammett] found it for me years ago in Chinatown," she replied, settling the transparent silvery cloud around her shoulders.

We sat facing the water. Philip's voice in the dark led the rest. He bloomed at night, coming alive in conversation. Sometimes his diatribes, in those soft furry tones, put down current pretensions, hollow trends—more rarely, he praised. Outrage was natural to him, but when he expressed appreciation in speech or essays, though it was always restrained by his strong rationalism, his sincerity and warmth made it seem like a reluctant declaration of love.

"The ferry is late tonight," someone said.

But there it was, appearing broad and dependable, its deck all alight like candles on a birthday cake. We could hear the comforting swish as it went on its way and the mock ferocious blast of its foghorn. In my imagination I could see the ferry pulling up to the dock.

How well I remembered our departure all those years before. My husband, my son, and I were leaving the island; the vacation was over. Our bags stood packed at the door and the house, unusually tidy, already looked unlived in. We were all in high spirits, a journey was starting, even though we were only returning home. When we arrived at the dock it was crowded. Although the ferry took off each morning at the same hour, it always gathered an audience. We abandoned the car below and stood on deck looking over the railing. It was a brilliant day and the island was garlanded in sunshine. It had been a good vacation we said to one another, the small annoyances and disappointments forgotten. And we promised ourselves to return next summer. But we never did—and the house was forgotten until many years later with the Rahvs, it appeared unbidden as a dream.

That night after the dinner guests had gone, we cleaned up and then gossiped, comfortably stretched out on the disheveled sofas. Theo kicked the shoes off her long narrow feet and Philip savored the last tidbits as though he had not already had a surfeit. His insatiable appetite might have kept him up all night but the rest of us were tired. Later, I lay awake for a long time between the cool damp sheets. Through the thin partition I could hear their bed protesting beneath the burden of Theo and Philip's titanic lovemaking, then Philip snoring, Theo's cough; downstairs the clock struck the hours erratically. As day began to brighten the windows, I heard the sea gulls cry and this visit merged with that other one long ago as time collapsed inside the white papery walls of the house and I was ushered into sleep.

After the first visit the house on Martha's Vineyard belonged to the Rahvs alone. No more ghosts from my past came to haunt it. Habit, a relentless killer, had disposed of those frail forms.

Three portraits of Philip Rahv are framed in memory like a triptych. They are over-life-size and they possess an obscure meaning only partially understood. The first, the scene by the well in Bridgewater, Connecticut, is flanked by two set pieces from the Vineyard. Theo, my husband, and I used to swim every day in the placid bay near the house. Although we all urged Philip to join us he continued to balk in his lairs: the book-lined study and the kitchen. One afternoon, looking across from the water to the beach, unexpectedly I spotted him, fully dressed, moving ponderously toward us dragging a kitchen chair. We all waved enthusiastically as though witnessing the takeoff of the first blimp. He appeared out of place, sitting stiffly on the uncomfortable wooden chair. Like a Dalí painting, his large form looked freakish outlined against the smooth stretch of sea, sand, and sky. After a few minutes, without any gesture in our direction, he got up and slowly retraced his steps back to the house.

I surprised the third portrait one evening coming downstairs at dinnertime. It was seen through the window on the landing: Philip seated motionless inside a blackberry bower. He was wearing a watermelon pink shirt that emphasized the duskiness of his skin and his black hair. His gross body and his massive head with thick features, shovel-shaped nose, large ears with fleshy lobes a shade paler than his face seemed to crowd the dainty trellis aglow in the setting sun. Framed by the blooming vines, Philip was a large animal—this time trapped in the natural filigree of a candy colored aviary. Again I was arrested by the expression in his eyes. Unaware of being watched they were unguarded, and I saw that they were weighted with a bitter intelligence and an extra load of human sorrow.

The Rahvs' house on Beacon Street was tragedy made material. From the start neither Philip nor Theo were at ease there. Although he was proud of it, its history, its aspect of erstwhile money and gentility was alien to him. I had the feeling that with his solid presence he was attempting to reduce its smugness by subduing it to his differing needs. But it remained strictly Boston Brahmin, despite his garish paintings and, inevitably, the addition of several new bathrooms. It was as though Philip and some glowering witch-hunting minister out of the American past were locked in combat. Philip was always foe to all pieties. "Bah! Phonies!" He would exclaim, disposing of them with a flap of the hand or a nudge. But the spirit of the house on Beacon Street was persistent. Theo resisted it too. Always loyal and admiring, she was attracted by the Philip of Greenwich Village, a leader of *Partisan Review*, the teacher who supplied her with those reading lists. Now she seemed depressed and bewildered by this return to her own roots from which she was, largely, a refugee.

My memories are of oily dark mahogany wainscoting and banisters, many floors, mostly empty, high ceilings, and deep window embrasures. The view across Beacon Street presented similar dwellings high stooped and dingy also. They were now boarding houses, and trash cans lined the sidewalk. Philip's house, though privately owned, had undergone a conversion too. In the drawing room, where characters out of a Henry James novel might once have decorously sipped their afternoon tea behind heavy drawn portières, Philip was ensconced with his whiskey and soda. Theo had made muslin curtains for the stately windows, but they were skimpy and looked like dowagers in miniskirts. Here Philip argued with other professors from Brandeis, Harvard, or MIT about the cult of illiteracy in contemporary literature and the abuse of freedom from censorship. "Dey tink sex is something clinical—something separate from human feeling," he said. "Dey think dey are shocking, dey are only boring and ignorant. Such naïveté! Such idiocy!" Theo listened reverently, her mouth with its faint mustache open as if to imbibe his truths. In the kitchen the crockery still crashed, and although the sound was fainter than in the flimsy house on Martha's Vineyard, the kitchen on Beacon Street being far away and the walls thick, Philip, once oblivious, now winced.

With his remove to Boston, his role at *Partisan Review* grew minor. Still editor, he mainly used his power of veto now. It seemed to have overcome his genius for the discovery of talent. His conversation grew more negative too. "It's no good—no good," he would reiterate on almost any subject. But his appetite for gossip remained undiminished. Again and again we heard about the intricate psychological difficulties of the Robert Lowells and stories about Mary McCarthy's latest marriage to an American diplomat in Paris. My husband brought him all the news he could gather from New York as though it were a house present, some cherries, or a box of chocolate creams.

The tragedy on Beacon Street reached me one September evening. I was alone at the time; my husband was in Europe on a business trip. I believe that it was Bernard Malamud's voice on the telephone that was harbinger to the disaster. The night before Theo had gone to sleep with a lighted cigarette. She was the only one in the big empty house and when Philip returned the following morning he found his home gutted and his wife suffocated in her bed. Of this scene I have two visions: one consists of a heap of black ashes, the shell of a house a crematorium urn containing the remains of Theo, her white velvet skin reduced to cinders. In the other, Theo's inert body is draped across the bed, her head hangs down over the side, her voluptuous mouth wide open, her black eyes shuttered. Dressed in a virginal white nightgown, she is Desdemona, and Philip, large and dark, is Othello beholding his wife's corpse.

One more view of him from that time came to me through the reports of friends who attended the funeral in

Boston. Philip, always so concealed, was now overcome by emotion in public. He could barely stand up and arrived at the ceremony supported on either side by Theo's daughters. I see them, two lovely caryatids, dragging his huge form, a grieving gargoyle, down the aisle of the church.

A few days later he telephoned to say he was coming to New York. I awaited him nervously. All my life I have been loath to talk of the dead to the bereaved. I remember that after my mother's death I had allowed my father, in my company, to remain lonely while I self-protectingly avoided the subject of my mother. But for Philip's sake I was determined to overcome my cowardice. He arrived looking much as usual, but I was startled to see that he had difficulty negotiating the stairs. He moved like a very old man. His bear hug was warm and so was his soft slurred voice with that thick guttural accent I had grown to love. When we were seated with our drinks, steeling myself, I started to talk of Theo's death. "No! Stop it!" he almost screamed, his heavy kind eyes in their black pouches alive with something close to hatred. "Never mention it to me—never—you understand— you hear me? Never!"

What had I done? What secret spring had been released? Through my long-time affection for Philip I had unwittingly invaded some dark private recess where I had no right to trespass. Aghast, I retreated and the evening resumed its course. Later Philip would come to talk naturally of Theo and her daughters, but in his presence I never dared to mention her name again.

The enigma of his behavior remains and the shadowy antagonisms in the house on Beacon Street are unresolved. Did the spirit of the vanished New England preacher prevail? In wrath, did it punish Philip? Was Philip, in some way, the stronger, Theo a sacrifice, and the wrecked house a symbol for his burning scorn of bigotry?

Following Theo's death Philip sold the house on Martha's Vineyard that she had left him. Soon after, off season and deserted, it also burned down to the ground. I have not been back to the island so I do not know whether that piece of land is vacant, a missing tooth in the semicircle of white vacation houses fronting the bay, or whether a new building has sprung up on the spot, an intruder on my recollections. They are jumbled together in the scrapbook of memory: children's parties, the plodding ferry, beach picnics, and Theo and Philip profiled like paper-cutout silhouettes that I have rescued from the flames.

Several summers later Philip visited us at our country home in Purchase. He brought Peggy Whittaker with him. She was a young divorcée and I knew that he was considering marriage again. He had aged, but his black hair was hardly touched by gray. He lowered himself laboriously down onto the sofa. He seemed contented here; he had always admired our house. Perhaps its rambling form and country furniture, worn with use by five generations of my husband's family, reminded him of some Russian dacha he had glimpsed in his childhood. Or was he merely impressed by the number of our old-fashioned tile bathrooms? "I wanted Peggy to see Purchase," he said, as though my husband and I were the caretakers of some tourist place: Versailles or Schönbrunn. But his eyes rested on us with affection. I examined Peggy carefully. Philip, now in his sixties, had said when he announced their arrival, "She iss just de right age, tirty-nine!" But Peggy appeared even younger. An instructor at some obscure college in Massachusetts, she looked like a high school student herself—the girl next door. Philip had attached himself to another indigenous American product. She was short and sturdy, built close to the ground. She had a very white smile, cropped gold-tipped hair, and tawny skin and eyes. When we were alone Philip asked me several times if I thought her pretty, as though he now doubted even the evidence of his own eyes. He had grown still more negative and was planning to cut altogether his connection with *Partisan Review*. "It's no good," he said. My husband tried to dissuade him but he stood firm. The magazine would fold or it would be supported by suspect funds. Money and literary merit were always antithetical to Philip.

At moments I caught him regarding me with approval tinged by regret. He had been appalled at the happy event of my becoming a grandmother and at the time had commiserated, "Poor Dorotea! It's hard to believe!" Once he had burst out, "You used to be very pretty when you were young!" These were the kinds of remarks his friends and mine resented. "How can you stand him? He's so depressing," they protested. But somehow I never minded his rueful insults, if such they were. I felt them to be proof of his affection for me and of his unflagging honesty. In recent years he had grown increasingly obsessed with thoughts of age and death. But his horror was generous, including those he loved as well as himself. He had told me that at night in bed he stayed awake pondering the ultimate problem of mortality and recoiling in disgust from his own body as though aging were a kind of creeping leprosy.

Peggy arrived for dinner in an apricot mumu. She was weighted down by an elaborate golden parure: a long necklace and dangling earrings that Philip had given her. They would have suited Theo. But Philip watched her with pleasure; he was like someone nipped by frost who finds himself in front of a warm hearth.

Of course, along with a new wife, he acquired another country house, this time in New Hampshire, not far from Boston. Philip and Peggy wintered in Newton, Massachusetts, convenient for the schooling of her young son. "Horribly middle class!" Philip had said about this suburban residence. "It's no good," he added, as though spitting out an unpalatable Howard Johnson's meal. So once more, the city man tried to make himself at home on New England soil. But something was wrong. On our first and only visit to New Hampshire I was surprised to find the house squatting humbly beside the road. Made of shingles, it was painted barn red and there was a collapsed look about its shape that reminded me of an overgrown chicken coop. In the rear a wire mesh fence enclosed a few dusty zinnias and some weakling vegetables.

Philip greeted us enthusiastically, almost with relief, but he soon lapsed into listlessness. Peggy, by contrast, seemed to be bursting with pent-up energy. When we were by ourselves, she exploded, "I can't get him to leave the house. He just sits all day and night—never writes a word anymore—hardly talks—see what you can do with him."

But we could do nothing. Peggy, my husband, and I went swimming in the "lake" nearby. It was shallow, tepid, and muddy, but we honestly admired the pristine lines of the white wooden church and the village square. "He doesn't even go to the post office for his mail," Peggy complained as we were driving homeward after our swim.

In the house I was happy to recognize some of the relocated abstract expressionist paintings. They were now like old friends and I welcomed them in this depressed atmosphere. Peggy discussed her Ph.D. thesis; Philip cooked. The saffron rice had not deteriorated, but he ate it with reduced gusto, while he and my husband discussed *Modern Occasions*, the publication Philip had started after his divorce from *Partisan Review*. He talked with more animation about forcing them to change their format than about the new magazine. "Where can you get money nowadays?" he asked. But at each suggestion offered by my husband, he grunted, "It's no good—no use," as though the will to failure had now been added to his habitual mistrust of moneymaking methods.

"If he gives this up too, I swear I'll bolt," Peggy muttered. "Look at him!" It was midmorning and Philip was sitting immobile by the kitchen window. He was still wearing his pajamas, bathrobe, and scuffs. His bulk was as unmoving as a statue as he stared morosely at the scraggly garden. Of what was he thinking? The excitement of the communist movement in his early days in New York City? The beginnings of *Partisan Review*? Or was he facing down the ugly specters of old age and death that were moving closer with the passing of each day?

On the back porch at night he revived somewhat. Ignoring Peggy's warning about his high blood pressure, he helped himself to another whiskey and settled back to receive the fresh gossip we had collected for him. But my mind wandered as I listened to the cicadas and my eyes followed the tiny flare of Philip's cigarette— also forbidden. Over the porch railing the blackness was total. Where was I? Was this Millbrook or Martha's Vineyard? But Philip did not rouse himself for the woodchuck and I missed the punctual ferry and the breaking waves.

On Sunday morning, our last day, Philip was almost cheerful at the prospect of his luncheon guests, Frances FitzGerald and Alan Lelchuk. He had filled us in the night before. "She iss very beautiful," he had said. "And smart. Her reporting from Vietnam iss good. He iss a professor and iss writing a novel about student revolt at Brandeis, and he tinks she iss a princess. Her mother is Marietta Tree and when dey visited her he told me Frankie had to show him what knives and forks to use. Probably a lie!" he added. "But it works; each iss something new for de odder. It won't last." But it was obvious that as long as it did Philip would relish his anthropological research.

When Frankie and Alan arrived, due to Philip's prologue

it was as though I had met them already. She was tall, blond, clear-eyed; he small, dark, and bearded. After he had been introduced to me, he asked, his expression earnest behind his spectacles, "Do you always wear blue? Why?" as though this useless data was of utmost importance to him. He was as inquisitive as a squirrel gathering nuts against the winter season. For Alan, everything was provender for a novel. Frankie, with her candid eyes, was, indeed, lovely. However, it was not until I caught Philip observing her attentively with open admiration that I realized that she reminded me of the young Mary McCarthy. Down the long corridor of years, was Philip viewing his love affair returned in a distant mirror image by the presence of this other young couple?

Alan deferred to Philip. He was both brash and humble, a disciple. But I kept wishing that the master had been the vigorous man I had met some twenty years before on that snowy night at the Kronenbergers'. *Modern Occasions*, too, was a dim mirror image of the original, seen down the same long vista of time. If Philip had been able to read my thoughts I'm sure he would have squashed them saying, "Bah! Who needs to turn de clock back?"

Not surprisingly, Peggy and Philip parted. The marriage had been brief and Philip moved away from the detested middle-class environment of Newton to a bachelor flat in Cambridge. On his rare visits to New York he described it to me: "It has a good view, high up, two bathrooms, its own garage, and lots of service—very modern." But it sounded lonely.

He died there, just before Christmas 1973. But because I never saw him in place, his end is not real to me. At times I feel that Philip is still alive and that I may run into him on the street. He will be deep in discourse, vehemently pushing and nudging his companion into the gutter.

Following his death I learned two secrets, as though yielded by the grave since I am certain that Philip would not have divulged them. It was said that in his will he left instructions to give his money to Israel. After a lifetime in the United States, where he had tried to take root through his American wives and his American houses, like an exhausted swimmer who ceases to struggle and, almost with relief, surrenders to the sea, Philip, weary at last, had turned away to sink into the depths of his past. And perhaps in dying he accomplished the blending he had sought but failed to achieve by living. His earnings and Theo's inheritance, handed down from her patrician ancestor John Jay, were transfused for the benefit of the Jewish homeland.

The other disclosure reaching me from the grave concerns his name. The man I had known for so many years was not Philip, after all, nor Rahv. That name had been assumed. He was, in fact, Ivan Greenberg.

Chapter Six

GÖTTERDÄMMERUNG

Although I learned to diagnose the symptoms of hero-worship in myself, it was new—one more jolt out of childhood—to recognize, objectively, the process in others.

The house of Frederick Dupee, Columbia professor and writer, and his wife, Andy, looked out from a pleasant valley onto a broad passage of the Hudson River. It was romantic, evocative of the past, but unlike the home of Stanley and Nancy Young, an Eastern temple, this place was indigenously American. Over the sweep of uncultivated land stretching to the river I could picture a band of Indians running toward the horizon. The Hudson was revealed in a large triangle between the cleavage of the shore. It had grown from the ribbon that bordered Manhattan Island to a body of water as wide as a lake. For some reason, in the fading light of dusk it reminded me of Mark Twain's Mississippi, and I expected a paddle-wheel boat to appear within the triangular vista.

The house itself was peculiarly American also, high-gabled, shabby but splendid, as haunting as the setting for a tale by Hawthorne. Fred Dupee, out of Wisconsin, for years a member of a group of New York City intellectuals, fully appreciated the romance of his home. The Hudson Valley still echoed with its history, fast fading, but audible to him who knew how to listen and see with his imagination. When he first became owner of the Rhinebeck house he had talked enthusiastically about his neighbors, descended from the original settlers, calling them the "river people." They sounded like water sprites, but when I met one of the species she turned out to be an octogenarian, wispy as a cobweb. He introduced her to my husband as though presenting a young beauty and escorted her ceremoniously on his arm into dinner as if she were the duchesse de Guermantes and he the Marcel Proust of the early Combray years.

This night, however, the leading player was to be of a different sort. Our host met us at the door and told us about a Mr. Tailor, whom we had not met before. "He is fabulous—you'll see. He has moved into the area—a millionaire many times over, self-made, now a top executive in utilities. He was born in Hungary and has Americanized his name. His parties are right out of the *Arabian Nights*, under a pink marquee, with enough champagne to fill an ocean . . ."

I had a vision this time of the Great Gatsby, updated and transplanted from the manicured Long Island shore to the Gothic wildness of the Hudson Valley.

The rest of the guests were known and part of the Dupees' customary entourage. There was Philip Rahv, editor and critic. His presence was always pleasing to me. Although he was as swarthy and bulky as a Russian peasant, he never ceased to seem inappropriate to the rural settings he loved.

That night the critic Dwight Macdonald and his wife Gloria were also included. Dwight, an enthusiastic talker, was a major-key accompaniment to the gloomy minor of Philip Rahv. While Philip muttered and groaned, Dwight insisted loudly and guffawed. He had a pointed grisly beard and animated eyes behind spectacles. His conversation cavorted and stamped; at times he reminded me of a clever jester imitating the capers of a billy goat.

Gore Vidal was there, looking aristocratic and disdainful, and Chanler Chapman, son of the renowned writer John J. Chapman. He carried his family tradition like an overpowering load, too heavy even for his strong shoulders. He might have been classified as a "river person," having been reared beside the Hudson he had never deserted, but he was taken by the Dupees as part of the usual blend. Dressed in blue jeans, he certainly did not resemble the now departed octogenarian "river lady" I recalled in her refined chiffon ruffles and heirloom jewelry.

There were others besides, unremarkable for a party at the Dupees', and I no longer remember which of the regular band they were. Fred led me up to Mr. Tailor, murmuring, "You're going to adore him. I have seated you next to him." Mr. Tailor was tall and handsome in a Slavic way. Only his neat navy-blue business suit and starched white shirt resembled an American banker's and made the plaids, reds, purples, madras, and corduroy jackets of the other guests look as disorderly and colorful as a neglected garden of common zinnias. Our conversation began inauspiciously with his proclaiming himself a "hawk." The Vietnam war was as necessary in his view as World War II, and the Communist threat there as dire as Hitler. I attempted to divert him into other channels, searching for the qualities heralded by Fred, but Mr. Tailor would have none of it. Surrounded by the retired army of the anti-McCarthyites, he was still fighting the Cold War. I seemed to see him limned against the red, white, and blue of the American flag. He was shouting now, "So you are one of those pro-Hitler types—an isolationist!—unappreciative of the privileges of your marvelous country! I tell you it's worth fighting for. I will never stop being grateful for the opportunities it has given me . . ."

I could only long for dinner to be over so that I could escape. Suddenly, in the middle of his tirade, Mr. Tailor paused and without preamble asked, "Which one is Dwight Macdonald? Point him out to me."

I searched the islands of tables scattered around the high-ceilinged drawing room, dining room, and entrance hall. Shadows lurked in dark corners filled with dreams and the hush of the past, not to be routed by the noisy garrulousness of the present company. I located Dwight shouting at his dinner party. He was sweating and mopping his bearded face with a napkin, but he appeared to be enjoying himself immensely as he countered all opposition with the fly swatter of his shrill words accompanied by his high-pitched laughter. After the ominous proximity of Mr. Tailor, Dwight looked as endearing as a boisterous child at a birthday party, and I wanted to supply him with a cocked paper hat and a cardboard whistle.

I indicated him to Mr. Tailor, who studied him in silence, drawing his heavy dark brows together until they met across his nose, and dinner being over I fled from his side. But I continued to observe him throughout the evening. He was growing drunk and more menacing, his dark suit a lone storm cloud. Later, as I was sitting with Dwight Macdonald, he approached. His step tipsy but determined, he stopped, towering before the unsuspecting Dwight. Mr. Tailor's glowering expression cut off Dwight's copious flow of words and his loud laughter. "So you are Dwight Macdonald," he said with cold fury. "I am going to kill you." And seizing him by the lapels he started to shake him, as though Dwight's considerable size were no more than a small rabbit's.

A crowd had gathered around. Dwight was pale between his whiskers and Mr. Tailor seemed to be rapidly growing larger. "I am going to kill you," he repeated. And in the moment before the two men, locked together as one, were separated, I believed him.

I watched as Fred Dupee, aided by some others, detached Mr. Tailor from the shocked Dwight and escorted him, fighting all the way, across the room, to the door through which he was ejected from the house. Dwight tucked his crumpled plaid shirt back into his trousers and reknotted his tie. Fred returned with profuse apologies. He had a look of bewilderment and hurt in his electric blue eyes, with which I could identify. I felt a new closeness to him and, strangely, some understanding also of the departed Mr. Tailor.

I sympathized with Fred's glorification of this man, so different from him and his friends. But the royal mantle he had bestowed upon Mr. Tailor did not belong to him; it was Fred's creation—in tatters now. As he continued to apologize to Dwight and me I was saddened by the thought that Fred would no longer be privileged to attend those parties beneath the pink marquee where the champagne flowed like the sea—and if he should, I knew that the tent would be merely the equipment of a parvenue and the champagne would have a bitter taste.

And what about Mr. Tailor? No less than Fred, no less than I, he too in his own way was a romantic. An outsider, he felt that his pile of gold was being tarnished by the hot breath of the intellectuals. Mr. Tailor had selected Dwight Macdonald as their king. And pricked by his ego, goaded by his own imagination, he was out to kill, like a bull at the sight of the red cape.

The party was over. I realized that the Dupees considered it a failure and, as a hero worshiper myself, I didn't know how to tell them what it meant to me. Outside the cool air was a relief. The dew-drenched grass extended darkly, immaterial as a shadow. The Hudson illuminated by a full moon was paler and looked more solid than the land. It was late August, and with the new season we would soon all meet again in the city. I looked back at the high-gabled silhouette of the house, trying to memorize its outline. It rose peacefully against the night sky. But the windows blazed and I was certain that were I to return within I would find a scene of destruction smelling sharply of fire and brimstone.

Chapter Seven

THE LETTER WRITER

For quite some time I have lived in a high-rise on a block of private residences, brownstones that have been converted so that, like human beings, each displays individual characteristics. One has a bulging bay window that resembles a middle-aged potbelly; its neighbor's façade is heavily bearded in ivy; and the strawberry-pink mansion on the corner, uninhabited for generations, is as lifeless as an ugly princess under a spell in a fairy story. Across the street, a church and its red brick parish house occupy most of the block. Season in, season out, a homeless man with bare scabrous legs sits before the main portal. The sound of my coin falling into his paper cup is a tiny chime, and occasionally, I overhear a pedestrian murmuring a prayer to the white stone Madonna standing in the cramped church yard planted with roses and a single apple tree. I think of thousands of feet that have pounded these pavements and have disappeared, as mine will, too, some day.

Only now, when I recall him for the purpose of this memoir, do I realize that my good friend, Charles Jackson, used to live on this street. He had purchased his house from the proceeds of his autobiographical novel, *The Lost Weekend*, a "best seller" about an alcoholic. After he and his family had moved to

Orford, New Hampshire, whenever he passed this area, he would point out his former home, with pride, saying, "that's the one." But since his death, about twenty years ago, this particular residence has been noteworthy, for me, only because in passing, I had glimpsed the prominent, fleshy nose of Richard Nixon in the parting of the lace curtains of the parlor window. I had forgotten that my friend, Charles Jackson, had stood before him on that very spot.

Even when we say, "I remember," the claim is often devoid of content, like an ungrammatical sentence without a subject. When I reminisce about "Charlie" with his youngest daughter, now an adult, although we are fond of one another, our memories are unshared. For her he is "papa," while the friend continues to elude me. But when I hear Schubert's *Trout* quintet rippling, melodious, carefree (a musical work introduced to me by Charles Jackson), I feel his presence resurrected from oblivion.

Now, years after Charles Jackson's death, I begin to understand the basis of our deep but ill-assorted companionship. Unlike passion, friendship has its reasons, and, perhaps, in uncovering these, I may atone for the disloyalty of my amnesia.

It may be only in hindsight that I believe that I "fell" into friendship "at first sight." It was at a writer's conference at Marlboro, Vermont, that I first saw Charles Jackson, and for me, he immediately became the focal point of the group seated in bucolic, bohemian informality in a field in front of a red barn. This scene may be inaccurate, also, engendered by the truthful lies of memory, but it cannot be erased. He was a small man, plump rather than stout, with smooth, appetizing, polished skin that reminded me of the shells of chestnuts I used to collect in my childhood. He had a bald pate (although, at this time, he was in early middle age); his faintly Oriental brown eyes were, at once, mysterious, innocent, and curious; his nose was pointed like a sandpiper's beak, made, I fancied, to ferret out odds and ends of gossip and human behavior, the raw material for his novels and stories; his mouth, beneath a neat black mustache, was round and sensual. He wore a freshly ironed pink Brooks Brothers shirt with a bow tie. His prim appearance contradicted what I knew of him: the drinking, homosexual encounters, and attraction to "rough trade." Rather, he looked the warm family man he was also, and the small-town citizen of upstate Newark, New York, where he grew up and which, in some sense, he never left. There was little in this portrait to draw me, and it is possible that, in reality, it did not do so on that hot July day, with its smell of baking hay and it aura of literature oddly transplanted, like a White Russian émigré who drives a taxi in some alien city far from his native Petrograd.

I am able to remember only two others out of the group, and I am glad to have known them because, today, I am aware that they both belonged to endangered species. Ludwig Lewisohn, a famous author at that time, was an ardent Zionist as well as a scholar of classic German literature, a combination rare among later post-Holocaust writers. He had a massive, dignified head, a flowing mane of white hair, an air of eminence that reminded me of a bronze bust of Beethoven in the "music room" of my childhood home. He might have been found enthroned, in stately fashion, on a bench that would be marked, with a commemorative plaque of fame, like Goethe's sitz-platz, located in the formal park of a European spa I visited during summer travels with my family. Instead, memory has placed him squatting on the prickly unmowed grass in Marlboro, Vermont, with the rest of us.

The other person is Vincent Sheehan, member of a breed wiped out by television's coverage of the news, in which technological immediacy has supplanted the roamings, courageous and romantic, of the lone journalist, witness to events in places throughout the world wherever action was hottest.

Yet, at the conference, it was Charles Jackson who presented himself as a gift, less obviously impressive than the other two; "Chaplinesque," rather than Goethe-like or swashbuckling Romantic, he who would prove to be my close friend.

Since our relationship dated from the time following the overwhelming success of *The Lost Weekend* and the film made from it, starring Ray Milland, I know, only by hearsay, about his prior life when he was poor, writing radio soap operas and teaching, when he could find a job since he lacked the proper academic credentials. But one anecdote he used to tell about those days stays with me because it characterizes his childlike fancy, his wistfulness, his unbridled ambition, and his acquisitiveness. Driving from New York City with his family to visit his wife, Rhoda's, parents in Vermont, they always passed, en route, three perfect eighteenth-century town houses, white shingle, with black trim and shutters, perched in a row on a ridge in the New Hampshire countryside.

"When papa is very rich, we will live in one of these," he promised his two small daughters and his wife.

As in the storybooks, the wish came true, for it was in Orford that I was introduced to the Jackson family. But true to its type, as the tale continued, the wish brought in its wake sorrow and frustration, for which the gracious colonial house was the setting. I remember, especially, Charlie's study, a bright, spacious room, with lavish moldings, his desk impressive enough to have been used for the signing of the Declaration of Independence, his pens, pencils, pads, typewriters, neatly arranged, were almost never touched, for in this aristocratic setting, he suffered a paralyzing writer's block. Crowded into a Greenwich Village tenement, with wife and babies, often unemployed and penniless, he had managed to compose many short stories and *The Lost Weekend* that changed his life, while in this lovely long-coveted home, he wandered idly from room to room. Was he halted by the first astonishing triumph, unable to compete with himself, or, just like the prophecy of misfortune, the *maledetto* in Verdi's opera, *Rigoletto*, did the old house harbor a curse? Charles Jackson seemed an outsider in his own home. Praising the scenic wallpaper in the dining room or the graceful arch of the stairs, he was more caretaker-guide than host. The sight of his two pretty, young daughters trudging up the hill towards home, in summer holding their prize of wild flowers, in winter, wearing ski suits—bright dots against the expanse of snow—were like illustrations from *Heidi* and *Hans Brinker and the Silver Skates*. They were possessions, also, yet Charlie, in his fashion, was a fond and sentient parent.

"I will always remember the sensation of holding in my hand that small infant's foot," he told me, with wonderment in his voice. "It was so silky, and somehow heavy, like a round stone washed smooth by waves."

Visits to Orford were often interrupted by Charlie's bouts of drinking. Sometimes, when he was locked inside his room, the life of the house would continue around him, as though nothing were happening; at other times, my husband and I would make a hurried getaway. But it was at Orford that Charlie indoctrinated me, through his record collection, into a new intimacy with music, including that quintet by Schubert, a leitmotif that has the power to this day to bring the past into the present. But reading was our chief link. We were bound together by shared admirations—fans; we retained the childlike ability to be totally absorbed, transported by a book. It was this, more than anything else, that attached me to this comic-tragic,

Chaplinesque man, in a relationship, less ardent than love, more stimulating than friendship.

When he was in New York City, Charlie often stayed with us. Again these encounters were subject to uncontrolled bouts of drinking. During one visit he disappeared for several days, and his wife, over the telephone from Orford, directed me to pack his bag and to leave it in the hall next to the front door, which I did, hesitating over a full bottle of sleeping pills. But I recoiled from the role of psychiatric nurse, and decided to include the Seconal along with his tidy shirts and argyle socks. In the afternoon the suitcase was gone and I breathed a sigh of relief. But I found the door of his room tightly shut. Although I knocked loudly and called out, there was no response. I went in. Charlie lay in bed, wearing pink pajamas, apparently asleep, but he was not to be roused. The bottle of Seconal, almost empty, was on the floor beside him; a few pills were scattered over the carpet like jewels spilled from a casket. When the ambulance arrived, they loaded Charlie onto a stretcher and I followed as they carried him out. I noted, in cold blood, that with his face partially covered by the hospital sheet, his prominent, bald forehead resembled the portraits of William Shakespeare. I was shocked by my own detachment, until it occurred to me that Charlie, had he been conscious, would have been flattered. I believe he would have chosen my notice of his likeness to the "Bard" in preference to the warmest compassion. I failed to tell him about my discovery and remembered the scene only after his death. Following a stay in Bellevue, Charlie, as usual, recovered completely and returned to living with renewed zest.

The miles between Orford, New Hampshire, and New York City separated us much of the time. One summer our families vacationed together on Nantucket, but communications between Charlie and me were carried on, largely through the obsolete function of letter writing. I see the long envelopes, fat with neatly typed pages, postscripts added at the end and margins were garlanded in afterthoughts. His signature, bold, round, legible, was a trademark like his small black mustache. The letters always began: *Chère Mme. Straus*—a jest between us—that was not altogether that, but, rather a homage to our mutual idol, the author of *Remembrance of Things Past*. Charlie and I had been delighted by the coincidence of my name with Mme. Emil Straus, friend of Marcel Proust, Parisian salon hostess, daughter of the composer, Halévy, and widow of Bizet.

In his copious letters, he waxed more brilliant than in conversation, face to face. I wonder sometimes today, when letter writing is all but extinct, if Charlie, a late practitioner, kept our relationship alive through this lost art.

One summer when I had been engrossed by Thomas Mann's *The Magic Mountain*, I received an account from Charlie of his stay in Davos, where he had been sent as a young man through the bounty of a wealthy friend. Sitting at my favorite spot for reading, in our garden, in the shade of a giant maple, Charlie's letter merged with the book. It is possible that this effect was deliberate on his part, because for Charles Jackson, literature and life were never altogether separate. Despite the heat of August in Westchester, I seemed to breathe the pure, thin air of the Swiss Alps and Hans Castorp, Mann's protagonist, became one with Charlie. Not only did they share their tuberculin bacillus, but the enfeeblement of alienation as well: Castorp symbolizing the attenuation and confusion of an era's end; Charles Jackson, the insecurity of a small-town American exposed, for the first time, to the sophistication and glitter of European society. From the remove of his invalid's balcony in the sanitarium, Charlie had observed a family of sisters and brothers, approximately his own age, tall, blond, beautiful, and aristocratic.

He had learned that they were white Russians in Davos for the skiing, and that they rarely mingled with the patients from the sanitarium. Despite his timidity, Charlie determined to meet them. Like a hunting dog on the scent, he informed himself of the name of each one of the glamorous sisters and brothers, their routines and rendezvous. He trailed them to the cafés in the town and, from his balcony, he followed them, as far as possible, with his gaze, along the road to the ski lift. He admired the casual fashion with which they carried their skis and envied their easy camaraderie. And when they moved beyond his vision, his imagination pictured them like demi-gods from Wagner's Ring Cycle, poised for flight on a topmost peak. At night, when he was enjoying his final open-air repose well bundled up under a black sky, crisp with frosty stars, Charlie listened to the orchestra in the ballroom of a nearby hotel, and, in his mind's eye, he saw the mythical family as they danced tirelessly into the dawn, everyone as unaware as the characters in *The Magic Mountain* of the upheavals that were lying in wait for them. Charlie, too, did not think beyond the next day when, perhaps, he would, at last, have the good fortune to meet the Russian family, so similar, in his fancy, to the Rostovs in Tolstoy's *War and Peace*. One morning, he managed to corner his prey along a path in the pine woods used for daily exercise by the patients in the sanitarium. He stopped the youngest and loveliest of the sisters, and overcoming his shyness, he struck up a conversation with her. Not long afterwards, he was dancing, blissfully, with the little clan to the latest jazz records he had brought with him from the United States.

Some of his letters went further back, to his growing up in Newark, New York. They told of the pettiness, meanness, the limitations of the inhabitants. But Charlie, with his writer's memory, was able to magnify into high drama the pleasures, fears, victories, and hopes of a small-town boyhood.

Among the last letters I received was one that differed from the rest, and I wish I had it in my possession now. But it is with his other papers and manuscripts in the library of Dartmouth College, a stone's throw from Orford. Perhaps, the letter might prove to be disappointing if it were reread after so long.

"*Chère Madame Straus*, I am writing this very late at night or, rather, in the small hours of the morning . . ."

I pictured him at his desk in his elegant federalist study. He had recovered from his writer's block, but this later work never lived up to his expectations. As he grew older, perhaps, his vitality was, at last, drained by his excesses and the high-wire act of his nature, both genteel and outrageous.

The letter began with domestic news: Sarah (his older daughter) had been home for the weekend, she would graduate in the spring; then, what? Charlie worried . . .

Sarah had her mother's personality, stable, literal-minded, but her dusky beauty derived from her father's side of the family. Although Charlie tried not to show it, Sarah was his favorite and he delighted in repeating her precise, unimaginative remarks. Kate, his younger daughter, was fair, with her mother's light blue eyes, but her father bequeathed to her his love of books and his warmth.

The letter went on to complain about his wife's stinginess. It was her Scottish blood. She refused to buy a new dress, even when he threatened to throw the old one into the garbage can. Sheila, their boxer dog, had had an unfortunate spat with a porcupine and her body had as many quills as there are feathers in an Indian chief's headdress. Suddenly, there was a change of tone. For several weeks he had been thinking about a work sparked by Pushkin's narrative poem, *Eugen Onegin*.

I am going to try it out on you, he wrote.

Had he been listening to the opera on his phonograph?

Or was the impulse fueled by alcohol? I visualized him, floating through the dark panes of the library window, flying above the New England landscape where nothing stirred, arriving at a *dacha* outside Moscow. Tatiana sits in her garden waiting for a response from the haughty, disdainful Eugen Onegin to her love letter penned through the night before. As I read on, I saw that I had been mistaken: The scene of Charles Jackson's poem was home, Orford, New Hampshire; the heroine, his own daughter, Sarah, the object of her love, an Ivy League college man. I had been aware that, in reality, Charlie disapproved of him. He had told me, "He's all wrong for her; too rich, spoiled, and sophisticated."

In her bedroom, Charlie's heroine is composing her declaration of love. In this version, the old nurse is Rhoda, who promises to mail the letter at the Orford post office on her way to the supermarket. The young man appears driving an expensive sports car wearing a blazer with a Yale insignia. His manner is cool, he considers himself superior to this inexperienced country girl. Following a trip around the world by plane (shorter than Onegin's absence abroad), he returns, in love, to claim the heroine. But it is too late; she is already married to an older man.

In his wildest moods, when Charlie was very drunk, he had the audacity to believe he was one of his favorite writers. Now in a reversal of things, the worshipper of literature, a living dybbuk, invaded the imagined person of a famous corpse. When sober, depressed, he would ask, "What if I have all the liabilities of genius, without any of its inspiration?"

As I came to the end of his pastiche, I saw that although the plot and rhyme scheme were modeled upon Pushkin's poem, this work belonged to Charlie, indigenous, the product of his own heart. Tatiana—Sarah's husband—had been altered in the trans-position. In place of the valorous general, in full military regalia, his broad chest decorated with medals and ribbons, there was substituted the mere suggestion of a human being. But in this blurred presentation, I was able to discern a familiar silhouette; short, plump, bald, Chaplinesque . . .

> Dear *Madame Straus*, let me know by return mail, what you think of this poem.
> My love, always. Your Charlie.

When the telephone rang, I was surprised to hear the voice of Charlie's agent.

"Charlie died this morning from a combination of alcohol and sleeping pills," he said.

His health had been poor for several months and he was living at the Chelsea Hotel in New York City, with a friend. He had not been alone in the apartment at the time of his death—was it suicide or sham? More likely neither; but rather his exhausted body could no longer tolerate the habitual doses. As I hung up, I felt more stunned and disbelieving than sorrowful. I could not give credence to the fact that Charlie was gone: This act had been played so often, and, always, my friend had been restored, rosy and energetic. I could not accept his death; later I missed him, sorely, and then the anodyne of forgetfulness set in. I do not even know where he is buried. But now that memory has revived him once again, his remains do not seem to be located in the dead community of a cemetery. His memorial is to be found in the papery conservation of letters, stored in a college library, a stone's throw from Orford, New Hampshire.

Chapter Eight

THE HERALDIST

What are little girls made of?
Sugar and spice and everything nice,
What are little boys made of?
Snips and snails and puppy dog tails—

> *—fragment from a nineteenth-century
> nursery rhyme*

The photograph, blown up over life size, reigned on a wall of the foyer of Lillian Hellman's apartment on Park Avenue. A monumental presence, it confronted the visitor upon entering. Long ago, a camera caught the image of a majestic black woman, dressed in a prim, starched Victorian shirtwaist, her gray hair pulled severely back; stiffly erect, she towers above a small girl child, dolled up for the sitting in party frock and white-buttoned shoes, who hugs the nanny's long, dark skirt like lichen to the trunk of a tree. Neither the passage of the years, nor the fame and sophistication of Lillian Hellman, playwright and memoirist, has dimmed the mythology of this pair: the regal servant and the "sassy" white babe. Yet the facts tell us that Sophronia was employed only briefly as wet-nurse by the Hellman family, and Lillian, as she grew up, was obliged to seek out her private oracle at the home of strangers, where two boys in her charge were oblivious to the homespun sage in their midst. An exaggerated shadow, the photograph followed Lillian in her various dwellings. And just as a woman noted for contemporary chic likes to cloak herself in threadbare costumes from her attic, Lillian Hellman masquerades in the feather boa fantasies of the South.

Yet, in the main, her home had been New York City and

she was the only child of German-Jewish parents whose family had emigrated to Louisiana and Alabama in the mid-nineteenth century. It is true that in her youth Lillian spent several months of the year with her father's spinster sisters who ran a shabby boarding house in New Orleans. Their antiquated standards and restraints sometimes clashed with the strong will of their hoyden niece, serving to enhance their sentimental value in the memories of the writer; for Lillian, a fight would always be more desirable than peace; enemies, more stimulating than friends.

On an evening in late May 1984, my husband and I dined with Lillian Hellman. A few weeks later she died at Martha's Vineyard, ending a friendship spanning more than twenty years. After paying my respects to the photograph of Sophronia in the hall, I entered the living room where our hostess greeted us from a red velvet Victorian settee. Too ill to rise, she was crippled, virtually blind, and suffered from emphysema, which did nothing to slow down the compulsiveness of her chain-smoking. That night, she was wearing a scarlet gown, cut low enough to reveal the subcutaneous mound of a pacemaker, like a new, miniature grave outside her heart. She had just been to the hairdresser and her long, swinging bob, in the fashion of a 1940 debutante, was freshly waved and dyed a brilliant golden blond. Her mouth, with its slash of lipstick the hue of dried blood, was an open wound, and her high-bridged nose jutted like the prow of a schooner from a face lined as an explorer's map. But the traces of Lillian Hellman's years of adventure were to find more prominent recordings in the pages of her memoirs. It is my belief, however, that she would gladly have traded all her success in exchange for the pretty kitten features of a belle, a white-pillared mansion, and an indigenous Southern lineage.

When we moved to the dining table, two nurses appeared, silently, to assist her. Dinner was served by a black woman, the last of a line that attempted to recover Sophronia. Our hostess, frequently racked by that shattering cough, nevertheless led the conversation, her wit as sharp as ever, if even more acid; her vocabulary tangy as a stevedore's, her laughter, robust like the cough, threatened the precarious assemblage of her body. I marveled at her fight and resented the attempts of a nurse to push food into her resisting mouth. But Lillian waved the fork away, absently, as though she were merely swatting an annoying housefly.

"Last winter in California was great," she told us. She had been the guest of one of those young male friends who attended her with the gallantry of suitors. "But I couldn't work on my book. I have very bad writer's block!"

So near to death and still able to complain about writer's block!

"Tell me about the book—" I began, but was halted abruptly. I had intercepted the glance of the black serving maid. Hatred, mute and murderous, was beamed at her employer. Was Lillian a difficult mistress, cantankerous, overexacting, or were those the poisonous rays of New York City's racial hatreds? This, then, was the conclusion of the Southern fable. For an instant, I was relieved that Lillian was unable to see.

Returned to the living room, I dodged the burning cigarette, removing it from Lillian's wavering hand and crushing it into the littered ashtray. But she had already inserted another into the gash of her lips, requesting my husband to light it for her. On a drum table beside me a Tiffany lampshade showered its stained-glass glow upon two photographic portraits in embossed silver frames: Lillian's mother and Dashiell Hammett, her lover, off and on, for about thirty years. The mother appears young in the picture, but her mild face is rendered insignificant by the elaborateness of her coiffure, and her body is disguised and deformed by bustle and stays; her bosom, capacious as an overstuffed cushion swathed in lace and satin. In the living room, no likeness of Lillian's father is to be found, although I had learned from the memoirs that she had been closer to him than to her mother. But as a salesman never quite able to provide adequately for his wife and daughter, he was excluded from the pictorial pantheon. One of Lillian's passionate contradictions would always be her love-hate relationship to money. Her most acclaimed plays have dramatized the maternal clan, their greed, ugly materialism, and their incessant squabbling about fortunes made and lost. Although she relates that at family gatherings she stood apart, disgusted, and despite the fact of her own considerable earnings and her luxurious lifestyle, wealth continued to attract her like an unconsummated affair.

Nowhere in her dramas is there mention of Jews. And, just as a set of Louis XV chairs is overlaid by paint, covered in tapestry, hiding the basic material beneath, these creations also conceal, denying in recall, the fine wood grain of genuine family history.

Willy, an uncle, the husband of her mother's sister, is a major gargoyle in her memoirs; he upholds the walls of their shaky genealogy. Sufficiently seductive to merit a chapter to himself in the pages of *Pentimento*, he is traditionally equipped with an invalid, drug-addicted wife, a retarded son, and mysterious Mafia-like business connections. The adolescent Lillian fell in love with him, almost—saved from actual incest at the last moment through some clever, "spunky," if nebulous, action of her own. The "Willy" episode would prove to be a prototype for her future amorous ambiguities; romance and outrage mingling, as they would, throughout her life.

One might wonder at the proximity of these two silver-framed photographs bathed in the prismatic, cathedral light of the Tiffany lamp. In contrast to the mother, the image of Dashiell Hammett is lean, keenly dark-eyed. An unregenerate Communist, he had been a Pinkerton detective, tough soldier, and the author of widely popular, cool, street-smart murder mysteries; and he was to play, throughout his affair with Lillian, the role of indispensable tutor. Their love was expressed, Hemingway style, waged through fierce physical combat, drunken scenes, infidelities on both sides, and hard-won reconciliations. Housewife-mother and apache-lover, I doubt they ever met, but they were linked through their photographs, forming two sections of Lillian Hellman's contradictory self-constructed emotional coat-of-arms, emblematic of proud old money and stubborn pro-Stalinist communism. A third part was occupied by Sophronia, African-queen nurse. Thus armored, Lillian, female knight, ventured forth, aggressive, yet questioning, forever in need of a mentor. ". . . Dash, show me how . . . Tell me what is right." "Sophronia, answer me. You know truth," the adult's plea merging with the treble voice of the girl-child from a past gilded by wishful visions of Southern aristocratic affluence. And yet, Lillian remained a staunch apologist for Stalinism long after her associates had fallen away.

"Bah," my friend, Philip Rahv, bitter anti-Stalinist, disillusioned Trotskyite, used to say "Wid Lillian it iss all romance. She was never political, not truly a Red. She tink she and Dash are Tristan and Isolde. Everyting iss in de imagination. She iss a romantic, tru and tru, forever revising de facts!" But his rough voice issuing from his bear-like person did not sound unkind. Rather, it reminded me of a shrewd country doctor who has just diagnosed an illness, chronic but not fatal.

His words returned to me on an evening in which Lillian and I were alone in her town house in the East eighties, near Madison Avenue. One of a row of similar façades, it was part of a residential block for the privileged. Now, when I pass that particular door, I seem to see her name permanently carved into the lintel. Perhaps it was in this home that she fancied she had recaptured an echo of her mother's early days of Southern cordiality while the Park Avenue apartment represented in her scornful view the displeasing conventions of New York City "nouveau riche." In her town house Lillian gave many parties. She was a good hostess who liked to prepare favorite Cajun dishes herself. A celebrity, she enjoyed collecting other celebrities who were attracted by her hospitality, her cleverness and humor. In the tasseled, portiered rooms one could find a cross-section of intellectuals, artists, musicians, politicians, tycoons and, of course, theater people. Despite her foremost position as playwright, there was always a note of disparagement when she spoke about Broadway.

"I enter the theater, young," she would say, "full of hope; but when I leave, I am hopeless and greatly aged!"

For Hollywood, even before the McCarthy era, she displayed nothing but the strongest of her famous venom. That evening we sat side by side on the velvet sofa, located then in the town house. We laughed a great deal and, as usual with Lillian, I experienced a sense of camaraderie that I mistrusted as soon as we were apart. Suddenly, she moved closer, her face so near that her features appeared alarmingly enlarged, distorted into a mask of rage.

"Do you realize that your husband is a malefactor?" she asked.

Stunned by the unexpected assault, I barely managed to inquire the reason.

But Lillian was launched. "He publishes Solzhenitsyn," she snapped.

"Surely, he has the right," I began.

"What right?" she interrupted. "What is right? Roger is wrong. Solzhenitsyn is evil; he is the Devil. Furthermore, if you knew what I know about American prisons, you would be a Stalinist, too!"

I felt bewildered, like Alice in the wake of the senseless tantrums of the Duchess in Wonderland. Were Roger and I about to join the swelling ranks of Lillian's enemies?

"It iss all Tristan and Isolde." I heard the voice of Philip Rahv again. And Fidelio, too, I thought. With Dashiell Hammett, Lillian Hellman had quaffed the magic love potion, in this instance spiked with communist zeal; later, like Leonora in Beethoven's opera, she had fought to free her beloved from jail. She supported Hammett in financial ruin until his death, and the opera curtain would fall only with her own end.

She must have forgotten Roger's crime, I mused, as we three sat in amity at that last meeting. Or, perhaps, it was another of those violent contradictions that Lillian thrived on, because I noted that she addressed him in that flirtatious manner she reserved for successful, masterful males; a Southern lady's subservience sugar-coating her own peppery aggressiveness.

I passed in review the antitheses in the scenario of Hellman's life: the willful tomboy, the well brought-up little miss, the daring reporter (Spanish Civil War and Russian front), the gracious salonkeeper, the suburban farmer, the veteran playwright nervously vomiting in the ladies' room on opening night, the good chum, the dangerous foe, the self-proclaimed heroine, the hero-worshipper, the witness, dramatically flaunting her right to take the Fifth Amendment while testifying before the House Un-American Activities Committee and wearing an expensive French import purchased especially for the occasion!

With that pseudo-frank modesty that was actually swagger, I had often heard her disclaim, "I was never brave, you know.
I would just ask myself what Hammett would want me to do,
and then I did it. I am really a natural coward."

When Roger and I moved to leave, the silent nurses
reappeared, as though radar-directed, to lead Lillian to her
bedroom rigged like a medical station on some other planet:
bells, light signals, wires, tubes, and tanks at readiness. The
antique double bed, from her mother's Alabama home, had been
pushed aside for the nurse's use. Lillian occupied a hospital cot
with mechanical devices that could bring her no ease.

"Stay a while," she begged. "I'll be ready in a minute."

We found her propped in her hospital bed, in a
coquettish short pink nightgown that revealed her thin, brittle
legs knotted by varicose veins. And just as butterflies may survive
the dead season at summer's end, two pink bows quivered on lace
straps that kept slipping down from her skeletal shoulders. Like
someone who averts her eyes from an accident, I turned away,
more in horror than in pity from this moribund frivolity. Her
conversation, however, continued animated, witty, and wicked,
interrupted by the blast of that shattering cough. The nurse
remained in the room with us, her silence expressing disapproval
rather than shyness. When at last we said good-bye to her, Lillian
clung to our hands.

"Don't forget that you are coming to visit me at the
Vineyard," she reminded us.

The heraldist is dead. The pieces of her escutcheon have
been scattered as illustrations for her biographies. Known for her
audacity, sexual liberation, an elder feminist with a combative
stance, a cantankerous partisan, she was, also, a woman of
paradox who yearned to claim as her own the background of an
upper-class, genteel Southern Victorian childhood. As I was

writing this memoir, a fragment of a long-forgotten nursery rhyme (quaint when I first heard of it, archaic now), presented itself as inscription for Lillian Hellman's blazon. The heraldist's dreams are romantic, incongruous, unrealized.

Chapter Nine

THE HORGAN PAPERS

The tall bookshelves in Paul Horgan's living room seemed to provide shelter against the record-breaking heat of August. Here, there was neither hour nor season, and a tempered light was filtered through the green glass shades of student lamps. My host greeted me from his habitual leather armchair placed in a snug angle of his library towers that reached from floor to ceiling. He apologized with genial gallantry for not rising (he suffered from arthritis, crippling and painful, and he had attained, recently, the age of ninety-one). As always, I noted the theatricality of his diction, with its hint of British accent, the grace of his speech, echoing the perfected music of his prose.

I felt that we (Paul, Don, his companion, and I) were players in a drawing-room drama, a touch obsolete, perhaps, but reassuringly heartfelt, humorous, and cultivated, in which Paul, the playwright, leading man and director, was also the appreciative audience. He wore a dapper, checkered tweed jacket with sporting elbow patches, a bow tie, and gray flannels. He had aged, decorously, during the years of our friendship, his cheeks unlined and rosy, his blue eyes clear, his salt-and-pepper hair receding, only slightly, from a high intelligent forehead.

Paul Horgan, born in Buffalo, moved with his family to

New Mexico, due to the ill health of his father. There, Paul attended a military academy; and just like a nimbus of an officer's uniform, an aura of pride in his country and a desire to serve still clung to him. He returned to upstate New York to enroll in the Eastman School of Music, with the intention of becoming a singer, but a *Harper's* prize in literature steered him toward writing. He remained, however, for all his life a passionate, well-informed amateur musician, as well as a painter who often used his watercolor sketches as notes for an incubating book. He authored nineteen novels, sixteen works of history, and other nonfictions and countless short stories. *Great River: The Rio Grande in North American History* earned him a Pulitzer Prize and, more recently, he was known for his stately biography of Archbishop Lamy of Santa Fé.

In old age, he had settled in this comfortable house on the Wesleyan College campus, in Middletown, Connecticut, a haven donated to him in recognition of his founding and directing of their Institute for Advanced Studies.

"I have been rereading Edmund Wilson's magnificent *Patriotic Gore*," he said now, leafing through the pages, again, with reverence.

Wilson had been at the Institute, and I recalled him exclaiming, "What a fussy housekeeper that Horgan was!"

I could picture the aging dean of critics during dinner, spluttering like a boarding-school boy with the giggles, as he pretended to hide his wicked mirth.

Had Paul been oblivious, or in the generosity of his admiration for the works, was he indifferent to the testy personality of the man?

Yet he could bite back, scorning what he considered merely modish, and in his *Approaches to Writing*, a collection of insightful jottings, aphorisms, and elegant essays in miniature, he stated, "The great lack of most modern fiction is any sense of inner life and meaning in the characters, apart from the motions they are put through. Numbed by behaviorism in its various forms, we are expert in catching the externals . . . technical actions, including sexual, but a cumulation of these, no matter how copious, all too often adds up to immense triviality. Imagine Tolstoy without his thought of God, or Maurice Baring, without culture—that sense of life above and beyond our lives which is the clue to our inmost nature."[1]

At times, despite his years of prolific, profitable output and the variousness of his expertise (perhaps because of it), he felt excluded from the intellectuals of New York City. "At seventy-nine," he wrote, "I am sometimes referred to as a 'man of letters,' always with a consoling tone implying obsolescence—as though the interest and practice of more than one literary mode were a quaint habit of a vanished age."[2]

Just as a statesman from the past may be commemorated on historical anniversaries, Horgan might be considered worthy but decidedly anachronistic in his own day. But at the Institute for Advanced Studies, surrounded by prominent novelists, poets, philosophers, critics, composers, and legislators, he reveled in his role of head steward to the reigning royals.

The late afternoon was growing cooler, and Don suggested that we "repair" (as Paul would have phrased it) to the gazebo, outside. It was only then that I noticed a wheelchair waiting at the door, unavoidable as a hearse parked before a funeral home. I shuddered as Don pushed it toward Paul, who dismissed it with a brave wave of his hand. Rising to his feet, with the aid of two

[1] Wesleyan University Press, 1968, pp. 73–88.
[2] Wesleyan University Press, 1968, pp. 73–88.

orthopedic canes, he hobbled precariously, through the living room to his bedroom, where French windows led to a small garden. Just like a tourist taken into the private quarters at Versailles, I was interested in the particulars of this intimate chamber: the bed surrounded by books—they were the courtiers who escorted Horgan to his rest at night. But I knew that the early morning hours of wakefulness were given to composing the next segment of a work in progress to be effected, punctually, at nine a.m. at his desk. *Tracings: A Book of Partial Portraits,*[3] was published coinciding with Horgan's ninetieth birthday. When we spoke on the telephone, I asked him what he was writing at the moment, knowing that he never remained fallow, but had several projects under way at the same time. I visualized the stacks of uncompleted manuscripts in boxes, like horses in their stalls, waiting to run.

"Essay or short stories?" I said, bowing to old age.

"Neither," Paul answered, and I detected an uncharacteristic shortness in his tone. "It's a novel, more personal, perhaps, than anything I have attempted so far."

A space in front of the window of Paul Horgan's bedroom was occupied by a *prie dieu,* and I wondered how his stricken limbs would permit him to kneel for his Roman Catholic devotions. *Prie dieu* and desk were linked, and like the guardian angels in a painting by an old master, they sustained and blessed his passing hours.

We sat around a table in the gazebo beneath a roof smothered in flowering vines.

"My distinguished physician is joining us for cocktails," Paul said. "I have spoken about you so often, and he is eager to make your acquaintance."

3 Farrar, Straus, Giroux, 1993.

I recognized this as a figment of Paul's chronically chivalrous speech, and when the guest arrived, he proved to be neither impressive nor eager. A young doctor, small, sallow, with weary dark circles under his eyes, he resembled one of the species of hospital residents seen hurrying along the corridors, a stethoscope peeping from the pocket of his clinical smock, like the white carnation in the buttonhole of an usher at a wedding. His wife, an active member of the local PTA, lost no time in praising the Middletown school system and her children's participation therein. But Paul Horgan had the capacity to make a fete from the meager ingredients of any gathering. It was Don's duty to replenish the drinks and pass the olives. He also drove the car, cooked, and managed the wheelchair. When not ministering to Paul's needs, he taught piano and played the organ in the town's church. Yet he appeared lethargic; a tall, portly, middle-aged man, he had a premature paunch and a boyish face with blurred, regular features, and he made me think, somehow, of a failed priest. It was Don who had built the gazebo and planted the small flower garden beneath the maples that shut out the active campus. When the telephone rang, Don left to answer it. At moments like this, one was forced to acknowledge Paul's infirmity; the thresholds of his home having become as hazardous as mountain passes.

When he returned, Don reported, "You'll never guess—that was Brigitta [the dancer whose stage name was Vera Zorina—a divorced wife of George Balanchine and the widow of a network tycoon]. She called to tell us that she was married today at noon in Santa Fé. She and her husband plan to live there, permanently."

Did I see a shadow crossing Paul's face, his clear blue eyes clouding for an instant as he slumped in his chair? Was he thinking that he might never see his friend Brigitta again? Then, like a military man, he squared his shoulders and holding out his glass, he said, "I propose a toast to glorious Brigitta, in absentia. May God bless her future" —adding, "I will call them tonight, to congratulate and to deliver my warm wishes, directly."

For several summers, Paul Horgan, Brigitta, Igor Stravinsky and his wife Vera, met in Santa Fé for the formation there of the opera company. Although the dancer had a secure place among Horgan's "royals," I knew from my reading of *Encounters with Stravinsky: A Personal Record*,[4] that the Russian-born composer-conductor held front rank.

Paul Horgan, a true hero-worshipper, was able to admire at a distance, to fall in love, so to speak, with someone he had never met. Imagination and art could trigger this special compartment of his personality. There had been Chaliapin and Greta Garbo, and a lifetime ago at the Eastman School of Music, Igor Stravinsky, elevated through Paul's intimacy and passion for his recorded music. He describes his first view of the conductor at the Paris Opera, where Stravinsky's *Petroushka* was being performed:

" . . . far away the low door under the stage apron slowly opened on a dim square of ochreous light, against which a figure moving with deliberate pace came in silhouette into the spacious orchestra pit at the station of the double basses, and slowly threaded his path between the first violin stands to the conductor's desk. This progress was assisted by an upswing of applause in a great draught like air hauled into fire. . . . The focused distance made him [the conductor] seem large, an impression heightened by his serious bearing. His face was pale,

[4] Wesleyan University Press, 1972, p. 89.

his glasses were fleetingly visible as they caught the light, his head was glossy and his features so strongly modeled that I felt power concentrated in that brief glimpse . . . he raised his arms and I saw his extraordinary hands . . . I could see their workman's squareness, even, I could say, builder's . . . the manual power and nicety of hands long disciplined in the craftly aspect of an art. . . . It was remarkable how even before the indicative upbeat the energy of his style could be felt. Then, like a powerful breath intaken, his right hand broke the air, using no baton—in the silent upbeat to be followed at once by a decisive downbeat, and the sparkling festival of the Russian village sprang alive in the horns and woodwinds."

Horgan's friendship with Stravinsky, begun in Santa Fé, grew in New York City, hero worship undiminished. The tiny, frail genius with avian features became a giant, and his childlike eccentricities were small wonders. Even those close to him shared in his effulgence. Vera, his wife, who wore the painted theater mask of former beauty, was remodeled by Paul in sincere hyperbole: ". . . the light of her dark-lashed eyes under blue-shadowed lids seemed to bring responsive repose into the assembly . . . and I said to myself, she is a moon goddess."

After the doctor and his wife had gone, we moved back inside, and the good conversation orchestrated by Paul caused me to neglect to consult my watch. When I did so, we all realized that Don and I would have to rush to make my train. A hasty farewell managed, nevertheless, on Paul's part, to be ceremonious. The road stretched ahead, we had a long way to go, and when Don and I arrived at the New Haven station, we were informed that the train to New York City had just pulled out. He refused to leave me in the waiting room, and we were confronted by an afternoon on the streets of New Haven. I had never been alone with Paul's friend, and he seemed, abruptly, a stranger. Without Paul, what would we have to say to one another? I knew that he was an executor of Paul's manuscripts and library, and during our long, hectic, mostly silent drive, I had been tempted to ask him about the new work in progress. I heard again Paul's tightened voice over the telephone, "It's a novel, more personal, perhaps, than anything I have attempted so far." I reviewed the many years of our relationship, in retrospect, elusive, transitory. What would this book reveal?

"This was the old library building," Don was saying now. "It's a very fine example of Romanesque architecture, but it's hardly used these days."

The streets of New Haven were derelict, even the homely landmarks of the college town of my youth had been razed, leaving decayed honky-tonk and shabby storefronts . . . an abandoned city, indeed inappropriate to an afternoon of tourism. But Don felt obliged to entertain me, and like a guide, as though we were viewing the beauties of Rome, he pointed out the sites. His tall, portly frame and classical profile, engulfed in fleshiness, reminded me, again, of a cleric without collar. I paid scant heed to his words, as I continued to ponder the undisclosed content of Paul's unfinished manuscript, which might never reach publication. Had Don been privileged to read it?

As though we were archaeologists bent on reconstructing in our minds the Forum, at a certain spot, Don explained, "This is where the Taft Hotel was located. There was no need for it. New Haven has spread and motels have replaced it."

We hurried through the streets as though pace might generate purpose. At last, I asked,

"Have you seen anything of the book that Paul is working on?"

Don made no response. Perhaps he did not wish to show that he was not a confidant, or did he find my question intrusive? It seemed indelicate even to me, but in my desire to acquire further biographical glimpses, I persisted; a detective in pursuit of a clue. Finally I gave up, and thanking Don for his kind attentions, I requested an early return to the station.

When the train, a pulsing beast, arrived, I was invaded by that sense of high adventure and sad partings that travel could engender. No matter that this rickety local conveyance was transporting me only between New Haven and New York City, and that from my window seat I watched the flight of industrial slums; I was carried back to the poppy fields and tidy, patchwork vineyards of the French countryside. At a stop I waited eagerly for the ham sandwich my father used to buy en route at some foreign depot. And so, from the sound of wheels on rail, space was consumed, and time dispatched, its orderly sequence disrupted. My visit to Middletown receded, merging with the memory collection of the past. I was not aware that this was to be my final meeting with Paul Horgan.

For months following his death, I averted my eyes from the shelves containing his copious writings and the generous gifts he had given me during his lifetime. I avoided the handsome set of Gibbon's *Decline and Fall of the Roman Empire*, my legacy from the dispersion of his library. Recently, however, just as someone whose wound is healing and who dares to remove the protective bandage, I took out the first volume, with Piranese's black-and-white views, somber and portentous as the tombs of antiquity. I studied Paul's *ex libris*: an open book, extended into a rectangle resembling the original image of the earth—above it hovered the gossamer wingspread of the letter *H*. The inscription to me in Paul's familiar hand reminded me, somehow, of his line drawing of the avian features of Igor Stravinsky.

I was no longer curious about the possible revelations in the unfinished novel reposing among the Horgan manuscripts at Yale. At that moment, through a kind of pagan ritual in celebration of the joys of reading, I had conjured up Paul Horgan in essential essence.

Chapter Ten

WOMEN'S STUDIES

Mary McCarthy was the intellectual "pin-up girl" for my generation. She flourished in the days before Women's Liberation became doctrine, venturing beyond the conventional limitations of her sex, while preserving her allegiances to homemaking and romance. In a time when beauty was acknowledged as necessary equipment for a female, a minor Helen of Troy, cool-eyed and sharp-tongued, she wielded influence, and to the envious, her face as well as her brains, launched her in her sure conquest of literary fame.

Our acquaintance stretched back to the 1950s, but with her last marriage to a United States diplomat, she moved to Paris and I saw her, rarely, after that. As I stood in the crush of mourners for her memorial service at the Morgan Library, I was unable to summon a strong souvenir of her presence. Sometimes death can be cheated of its finality through recall, the only redress against extinction available to the non-believer. But on that day, in the late 1980s, Mary McCarthy's seventy-eight years of heightened existence had already begun to dwindle and pale in my remembrances—they were remote, dead indeed. Along with other friends and relatives, I pushed my way toward the auditorium, hoping that a eulogy, someone else's memory, might revive her for me. But, at last, it was announced that all seats, as well as standing room were filled. The doors closed, and like fans turned away from a popular film, those of us remaining outside were ejected into the uncaring, quotidian November afternoon.

I walked up Fifth Avenue, taking pleasure in the first nip of cool autumn weather, the season of renewal in New York City. At the end of the canyon of buildings the hazy horizon of treetops in Central Park was as unsubstantial as my image of Mary McCarthy. —Indistinctly, I glimpse a cluster of literary and political literati convened in a room in Greenwich Village. I cannot distinguish their faces through clouds of smoke, but a hubbub of voices reaches me. The name of Trotsky is evoked again and again by a ghostly chorus of waning Marxists denouncing Stalin and Communism in bitter, disillusioned unanimity that has, nevertheless, the ring of clashing arms in a field of battle. In their midst, a silhouetted figure, seen in profile, sits in a rocking chair. She has a firm jaw and her dark hair is drawn back, severely, gathered into a tight bun at the nape of her neck. Who is this woman strayed into a den of males (mostly Jewish Eastern European intellectuals)? She is Mary McCarthy, out of the Pacific Northwest, adopted by the founders of *Partisan Review*.

Now, I sight her on a beach on Cape Cod. She is spreading lunch from a picnic hamper. The sky is pure, the dunes serene, the ocean embroidered in frilly white caps, gulls strut, circle, swoop—a picture postcard summer day; no more perfect than the alfresco meal prepared by Mary McCarthy. Had I been present at this scene, or did I only hear about it, or find it in a book? Just as a patchwork quilt is composed of scraps of material sewn together to make a whole, a memoir is a blend of hearsay and fact.

There is Mary, again, descending the bare boards of the narrow staircase in the upstate home belonging to Philip Rahv, her former lover, the Russian-born critic. It is New Year's Eve and the creaky Revolutionary farmhouse is cold and drafty. The celebrants would be happier in the overcrowded, smoke-filled room in Greenwich Village. Mary McCarthy is wearing, as for a gala, a long, red, white, and blue evening gown, a Parisian creation, one bare shoulder exposed to the chill drafts lurking around loose window frames and dusty corners. Although she holds no torch and her impudent, lively Irish beauty bears little resemblance to the calm, classical Grecian ideal of womanhood, as she moves down the stairs, she reminds me of the Statue of Liberty in motion. Years have passed since her liaison with Philip Rahv, much drinking and many random sexual encounters, culminating in a disastrous marriage, and divorce, Edmund Wilson. Photographs from the period of their union show him "older" (in his forties), appearing disheveled as in a perpetual hangover.

"Some women are more attracted to ink than blood," Philip Rahv had remarked. But as she comes down the stairs, he watches her from below, and his heavy-lidded dark eyes devour her.

She emerges from an automobile, shining and new, a Mercedes-Benz. She is older, now, and has lost some of her glow, but her convictions and enthusiasm remain vigorous. While devoted to prestigious foreign brand names, Mary continues to preach a litany in praise of tried-and-true indigenous American products, untainted by preservatives, "built-in obsolescence," and trashy synthetics.

At dinner in her apartment in a brownstone on New York's Upper East Side, she points out to her guests a painting by Max Ernst, a gift from the art collector Peggy Guggenheim, while her third husband busies himself with cocktail glasses and empties ashtrays.

• • •

As I proceeded up Fifth Avenue, I passed in review some of Mary
McCarthy's writings. Perhaps more than these scattered pictures—
like rooms exposed and partially furnished after a fire has
destroyed the connecting walls and doors—her books might
restore her. But the novels and short stories, though often
brazenly autobiographical, are unrepresentative. On the subject
of aesthetics, she seems to write in a language diligently learned
but never quite mastered; in her essays on literature and politics,
her voice is clear—her approval is lucid, her condemnation,
devastating. Mary McCarthy can destroy in a single thrust. Yet
she was capable of lifelong loyalties: Her idolizing of Hannah
Arendt, the German refugee, and Nicola Chiaromonte, Italian,
philosophers of history, verged on schoolgirl crushes. Constella-
tions, they neither flickered nor waned.

For me the most unforgettable of McCarthy's work is
Memoirs of a Catholic Girlhood. Here, with candor and no
self-pity, she skillfully evokes a past deprived as that of a Dickens
character. She came a long way from those childhood days; but
just as traces of penmanship learned in primary school may be
found in the handwriting of an adult, the hardship of those early
years shaped her future values and her insecurities, fueling her
ambition to be first. She and her three junior brothers were
orphaned during the influenza epidemic of 1918. Their youthful
parents contracted the disease on a train taking the family from
Seattle to Minneapolis, the hometown of the newly rich, narrow,
fanatically Catholic McCarthy grandparents. The children were
boarded with a heartless great-aunt and her gross, sadistic husband,
a freak. Grotesques—this childless couple cultivated ugliness and
parsimony as virtues, and subjected their wards, daily, to what
newspapers expose today as "child abuse." Mary survived by
assuming a stoic's mask of indifference, too proud to show her

hatred and impotent rebellion. At early puberty, she alone (for some unexplained reason) was rescued by her maternal grandfather, a respected Presbyterian lawyer in Seattle. Here the nightmare ends, but not its effects, and Mary would remain embattled. She wrestled with her early restrictive Catholic indoctrination, yet she quarreled with her doubts, while taking pleasure in shocking the benign convent priests and nuns she met along her path of war. Even after she had moved from convent to public school and then to a private, snobbish Protestant girls' institution, Mary continued to query herself, relentlessly, on the articles of Faith and the definitions of Right and Wrong.

The final chapter of *Memoirs of a Catholic Girlhood* is given to Mary McCarthy's Jewish grandmother, a cold, withdrawn woman from an alien milieu. For Mary, this grandmother was a subject of interest, mainly because of the feminine luxuries surrounding her. "I did not love this strange lady—but I loved the things she had," Mary wrote in her *Memoirs* years later. And she often accompanied her grandmother on her daily afternoon shopping expeditions, a ritual as undeviating as Catholic Mass. Mary was awed by the emporiums dedicated to feminine extravagance and she fingered the rich fabrics and studied the latest fashions brought out for her grandmother's approval. But as Mary trailed in her opulent wake, she wore, like a worn garment, the sensitive epidermis of the orphaned child, a poor relation.

By this time, I had arrived at midtown. At Elizabeth Arden's Beauty Salon the door opened its scarlet wooden lips to admit a customer into the street. As she brushed by me and from inside the store, a perfume common to these establishments for women the world over teased my nostrils. The fragrance, sweet, sensual, faintly decayed, like dying flowers, carried a message this afternoon. Unexpectedly, abruptly, I felt Mary McCarthy by my side—real at last, from her pepper-and-salt waved hair, bobbed now (the prim bun having given way to modishness and middle age), to the tip of her imported Italian leather pumps. We were standing on the threshold of the Lanvin store in Paris, where a fashion show was about to begin. I would have preferred to spend my last afternoon in Paris revisiting my favorite haunts, but Mary had insisted: "You must come with me. We shall have such fun."

I hesitated at the entrance, invaded by that sweet, hothouse odor. For no particular reason, I answered, "I'm not going to buy anything."

"As you please," Mary said. Although the glance of her gray-green, narrowed, observant eyes was friendly, I noticed, as I had often before, that her broad smile appeared weirdly detached from the rest of her person, reminding me of the free-floating malicious grin of the Cheshire Cat in *Alice in Wonderland*.

We entered the store and the fragrance of wilting flowers grew more insistent. But at this point, memory plays one of its tricks and, at a wave of a scented conjurer's handkerchief, the white, gilt-trimmed, multi-mirrored decor, the pale satin upholstery, uniform decor of such places, vanishes and, instead, I see a shabby eighteenth-century French salon with a pink marble mantle and dark, dingy plush chairs and sofas.

Mary McCarthy was greeted obsequiously by a salesperson, correct in a simple black dress. She was all honey: her neat coil of hair, her makeup and her tone of voice. It was obvious that a renowned author was a favored customer, here among the bejeweled matrons (few of them French) and the hard-headed commercial buyers. At the Lanvin showroom, Mary McCarthy was royalty, and as such a certain dowdiness was permitted; a slip showing, legs, sinewy and slightly bowed. We were directed to choice seats in the front row to watch the models glide by in their showcase. But the wrong lantern slide of memory refuses to be dislodged.

On our brief visits to Paris, my husband and I always stopped at the Hotel St. James and Albany. I became intimate with our room there, located in the old wing, once the residence of the family of Madame de Lafayette. I felt a proprietary affection for the grand staircase that led to the mezzanine, where an oversized key opened the door that, like a theater curtain, disclosed a familiar stage set: an eighteenth-century French salon, where two brass beds, makeshifts, floated in waste space, surrounded by the original theater properties, the shabby dark plush furniture and pink marble mantlepiece, that I have given, irrationally, to the Maison Lanvin. When I came inside from the streets veiled by a fine mist of déjà vu, our hotel room greeted me like an old friend. My feeling for Paris is dual: More than any other foreign city, it attracts me, but just like a bashful lover who, despite many rendezvous, remains at a distance from the object of his infatuation, I experience, there, a melancholy sense of exclusion.

On this visit I had no time to be lonely. The telephone in our room rang often and it was usually Mary McCarthy. Her voice over the wires was flatly American and her French, though fluent, was as accented as the greenest tourist . . . after all her years in Paris, she was too honest to attempt borrowed colloquialisms, or espouse alien ways, and she did not frequent the undiscovered "little places" favored by her compatriots. Mary was her unchanged self; only her attentions to me were new. And she would ask, ". . . luncheon at the Brasserie Lipp?" or "Les Deux Magots?" . . . dinner for the four of us at Maxims? or a party at her apartment on the rue de Rennes.

Earlier, when Mary was in New York on her way to rejoin her new fiancé, whose diplomat's post was then in Poland, she had boasted: "You will adore him. Every woman falls in love with him. He is the kind of man who looks as though he were about to kiss the hem of your skirt!"

In my mind's eye, I saw the first act of Verdi's opera, *La Traviata*, with Alfredo on his knees pressing ardent lips to a flounce at the bottom of Violetta's belle époque ball gown. In late middle age, Mary McCarthy, a no-nonsense critic, a sharp political thinker, a war reporter who would soon go to Vietnam, was also an assertive Romantic.

But at the news of this fourth marriage, Philip Rahv ran his hands through his tousled black hair, barely touched by gray, exclaiming, "It iss unbelievable! Why must Mary always marry? I tink, deep down, she iss still a Vassar girl, class of 1933!"

This time, the marriage lasted, and she made her home in Paris, where years later, I enjoyed this welcome. We would sit in the Luxembourg Gardens, chatting, gossiping, laughing wickedly at the foibles of others. Now I was able to watch the French boys and girls at play without the residue of envy I had harbored since my childhood travels with my family, when they had appeared as small prodigies, adept at the musical performance of their native language. How nimble they were at rolling hoops and sailing toy boats in ponds, and how I longed to join them in their games. But I never surmounted the sightseer's status. I had even suspected that the old women in rusty black (mourning for relatives killed in the First World War) regarded us with scorn, as they collected the coins permitting us to sit on the hard metal chairs in the gracious, shaded parks of Paris. With Mary, I contemplated with unmixed pleasure the beauty of the Luxembourg Gardens, where nature was trimmed and ornamented to make a playground fit for courtly dalliance.

At Lanvin, the final exhibit had arrived: the bride in dazzling white followed by the long satin comet of her train. As the final rocket on the Fourth of July, a splendid cascade of light, proclaims the celebration over; this designer's extravaganza closed the fashion show. The honey-voiced saleswoman reappeared, but before she could utter a word, Mary McCarthy introduced me, saying: ". . . she is my friend from New York City, and she wants to try on some of your beautiful models."

My disproportionate outrage rendered me helpless, mute, as I was led, unprotesting, into a fitting room. When we left the store, I was the owner of a spangled shirt, a detestable object I knew I would never wear.

In the street, I regained my voice. "How could you?" I spluttered. "I told you, before, that I was not going to buy anything."

"Then, why did you?" she asked, the smile of the Cheshire Cat, turned tigress, hovered between us. "Here is my situation," she continued. "I cannot afford Lanvin clothes until my royalties are due, and it makes me uncomfortable to just sit there—one must make a good impression on the sales woman."

Was it possible that Mary McCarthy had been oblivious to her reception? I smarted at the thought that I had been used as a decoy.

"I can't understand why you should be so angry," she continued. "It was certainly providential for me that you were passing through Paris at just the right time."

As folk songs were theme music for the "flower children" of the sixties, Mary McCarthy was known for the frank harshness of her speech.

Her words of introduction returned, but substituted for ". . . my friend from New York City . . ." she seemed to be saying ". . . my Jewish grandmother from Seattle . . ." Did Mary McCarthy associate me with that woman from an older generation, and those long ago shopping tours? Had she placed the cloak of her ancestor upon my resisting shoulders? It was useless to remind myself that to her adolescent eyes, this relative had appeared glamorous, to be envied. I held a different view. During my growing up in New York City in the late twenties and early thirties, my family, assimilated Jews, worried obsessively about social anti-Semitism. My mother, who abhorred everything ostentatious, believed that the compulsive consumer (if she were one of our kind) was a female stereotype, less virulent, perhaps, than the male usurer, but like him, a cause for the prejudice that from the enclave of our home, we dreaded. For me, as well as for Mary McCarthy, the past was not lost. Like baggage hidden in the hold of the subconscious, it waits to be reclaimed along the carrousel of chance.

ABROAD

Chapter Eleven

IN THE MEDICI WOODS

The Piazza del Popolo is unimpressive by Roman standards: the church, modest, no fountain boasting exuberant marble gods and goddesses, and the multi-layered evidence of the centuries is inconspicuous here. A short, steep incline between ivy-covered walls rises directly behind the Piazza, it leads to the Medici Woods and the studio of Carlo Levi. These unspectacular landmarks speak to me of the passage of time and mortality, more forcefully than all the tombs of antiquity along the Appian Way.

I induce Carlo Levi's image, in place, as inanimate objects unlike the mobile human face are fixed in memory. The studio has white-washed walls and a high ceiling, the furniture is sparse and comfortably worn. Everything is faintly permeated by that workman-like smell, an amalgam of paint, turpentine, and new wood, but in the homey confine of his studio I catch no echo of the timbre of Levi's voice. A ladder mounts to a platform under the eaves, a single window opens to a thicket of slender bamboo trees (from the distance of years, they appear in perpetual leaf). This rustic dwelling in a patch of sylvan, fairy-tale property belonging to France, was given to Carlo Levi in recognition of his painting.

His bulky body comes first, in silhouette, reminding me

of my initial glimpse of Rome: the massive, classical columns of the Pantheon, seen from a taxi at night, en route from the airport. His face emerges gradually, calm, broad, with aquiline features both kindly and archaic, topped by a thatch of thick, curly, iron-gray hair.

Carlo Levi's welcome was always warm; he possessed, in generous measure, the gift of friendship. No matter whether my husband and I found the studio filled with guests, or we were received alone, our host's attentions were invariably personal, beneficent, healing as a poultice. Actually he had earned a medical degree, years before, in his native Turin, and although he never practiced, his serene wisdom constituted, for me, a type of physicianly ideal.

Good conversation and leaden, soporific food competed with one another inside the studio. The afternoon was at its height before we climbed the ladder to the landing beneath the eaves where the laden table awaited us. The meal was interrupted, constantly, by the ring of the telephone, attesting to Levi's many friends. And just as a restaurant piano accompanies a hotel repast, the reiteration of "*Pronto*" punctuated lunches at the studio. We were served by a rough-hewn housekeeper who waited on her master with tender respect, never forgetting to address him as "Signor Senatore."

Carlo Levi's capabilities were manifold: painter, writer (author of the renowned *Christ Stopped at Eboli*), communist senator, genial man-about-town. He moved through his various worlds with unruffled equilibrium, and all manner of people rejoiced at his presence.

My introduction to Rome was in 1961, at the Christmas season, and Carlo Levi was chief guide. He showed my husband and me, not so much the anticipated works of art, but rather, the living, unexploited Rome. I remember in particular the *bécasse* hanging head downward, claws tied, in the drizzle outside the butcher shops. The diminutive birds are sold as holiday delicacies, but to my view, they were pathetic corpses in this city of violent contrasts, where signs of mortality mingle everywhere with the bloom of vitality. Palms and orange trees flourish in the dead of winter, in the spring wild flowers push their frail heads between the crevices of the ruins on the Palatine Hill, citizens, undaunted, make their homes inside ancient fortifications, putting out the scarlet pennants of potted geraniums on crumbling ledges, the severe hilly horizon is frilled by umbrella pines, resembling unfurled *Belle Epoque* parasols. And just like the healthy flesh of young Latin beauties, old walls glowed rosy and golden, even on that sunless Christmas Day. Sometimes Carlo Levi marched ahead, or we squeezed into his tiny black automobile that fitted his girth as snugly as sausage skin.

We lunched in an underground cave (a relic from the era of Julius Caesar), a working people's eating place, where the owner greeted Levi like an old friend.

"*Buon Natale, Marco,*" Carlo responded. "How is the family?"

"Well, Maestro, *Deo volente,* may they remain so. I would like to ask a favor of you. My oldest daughter has painted some pictures, but she is too shy to show them to you. May I do so?"

The bearded proprietor returned, dragging a reluctant young woman.

"Giuilia, show the Maestro what you have done."

One by one, the paintings were propped against the back of a chair. Carlo Levi scrutinized each one as gravely as a dealer judging a possible acquisition. His napkin still tucked under his chin, he had parted, with some reluctance, from his knife and fork.

Later that afternoon, ignoring the fact that it was

Christmas, he took us to see the oldest synagogue in Rome in the city's ghetto. Levi espoused no religion, but he knew his way around these narrow streets where tall, dingy walls created an everlasting night. Ragged children with old, sad, wizened, pale faces, preserved, it seemed, from the Middle Ages, follow his steps. He was a familiar here; a portly, aging Pied Piper with a benign, archaic face, he spread a swath of warmth where there was only damp and chill.

Through the years, on our visits to Rome, the hours spent with Carlo Levi increased and firmed the friendship. Knowing him made me feel that I was beginning to penetrate this unfathomable city; although after that Christmas Day, we spent more and more hours inside the studio. Season in, and season out, willing prisoners, we watched the mid-day light change to evening in the bamboo woods outside the window, while our host continued to talk in his unhurried fashion—and we learned to disregard the forward movement of our watches. Undistracted by the fullness of his days, Levi found ample time for everyone and everything.

One evening, we accompanied him to a party given by Princess X. I wondered whether her home might resemble the Farnese Palace. It was there Levi occasionally picked up his mail, parking his black beetle car in front of its magnificent Renaissance façade. I never asked about this odd procedure; perhaps it was a leftover from the Fascist regime, when the building might have been used as an unsuspected covert drop by enemies of the State. Or had the dignified palace been reduced, now, to a general post office? The latter thought was as disturbing as would have been the information that the white-haired old man who operated our hotel elevator was once a ruling noble. I looked forward to observing Princess X and her circle; they might afford a glimpse into the life of the ongoing Roman aristocracy. We drove through the Borghese Gardens, and it must have been spring because the magnolia trees, like festive candelabra, were in full bloom. But our destination turned out to be a modern concrete condominium, extending, disrespectfully, into the gracious Gardens, utilizing the surrounding greenery as though it were the parvenu planting belonging to an expensive resort hotel in Florida.

The Princess proved a disappointment also: Overdressed and bejeweled, heavily made-up, her voice, like a badly tuned violin, was an inadequate instrument for the mellifluous Italian language. Throughout the evening, she never ceased to flirt, unabashedly, with her handsome young butler; later I discovered them embracing in a corridor. At dinner, Carlo was placed to the right of his hostess, a seat of honor accorded to the ambassador from the realm of Art. I watched him enjoying the guests (new money and old titles) and the succession of rich courses and vintage wines, and I fancied that I saw a tipsy laurel wreath crowning his iron-gray curly head.

Life's turning points arrive when least expected. Carlo Levi, an Italian rebel, was released from jail in Rome and banished for a year to Calabria, in the southern tip of the mainland. Here, he met an experience that engendered his memoir, *Christ Stopped at Eboli*, a classic during his own time, on both sides of the Atlantic. The book appeared in 1947, and in 1992, Farrar Straus Giroux published a twenty-third printing. In an introductory letter to the English edition, Levi wrote:

> Many years have gone by, years of war and what men call History. . . . in a world apart, I am glad to return in memory to that other world, hedged in by custom and sorrow, cut off from History and the State, eternally patient, to that land without comfort or solace, where the peasant lives out his

motionless civilization on barren ground in remote poverty, and in the presence of death.

"We're not 'Christians,'" they say. "Christ stopped short of here, at Eboli." Christian in their way of speaking means human being, and this proverbial phrase that I so often heard them repeat may be no more than the expression of a hopeless feeling of inferiority. We are not 'Christians,' we're not human beings; we're not thought of as human beings, but simply as beasts, beasts of burden; and even less than beasts, mere creatures of the wild . . .

In Lucania, as an exile, Carlo Levi was enlisted to treat the ill, and the people clung to him, despite his hesitation to assume responsibility without experience. Their confidence in his powers and his rapport with them reduced the inadequate local doctor to the position of assistant. In Lucania, he befriended all: the "witches," bandits, fellow exiles, priests, but, especially, the peasants who eked, without protest, their meager yield from the barren soil. His painter's eye discovered beauty in the rocky terrain and the primitive dwellings growing like excrescences from the bare flanks of mountains. The movement of clouds, the change of seasons came to be action enough for this city person. A twentieth-century man of learning, he was able to accept the practice of magic spells; an atheist, he felt no revulsion before the doll idol of the Black Madonna of Viaggio, worshipped in every home.

To the peasant, everything has a double meaning. The cow-woman, the were-wolf, the lion-baron and the goat-devil . . . People, trees, animals, even objects and words have a double life. Only reason, religion and history have clean-cut meanings. But the feeling for life, itself, for art, language and love is complex, infinitely so. And in the peasants' world there is no room for reason, religion and history. There is no room for religion because to them, everything participates in divinity; everything is actually, not merely symbolically divine. Christ and the goat, the heavens above and the beasts in the fields below, everything is bound up, in natural magic . . .

When I read *Christ Stopped at Eboli*, I saw Carlo Levi as a latter-day Jupiter in the guise of a mortal as political exile, circulating incognito, among the humble natives of Calabria. In the post-*Eboli* years when I knew him, he was more author than painter. Once in a while, he did bring out a canvas to show us, but his subjects were, exclusively, the peasants of Lucania (painted from memory)—chiefly the women, young and old, strangely alike, with great round eyes like lumps of coal sunk into emaciated faces, their stooped shoulders draped in black shawls. The portraits of Romans, from all walks of life, his livelihood before exile, were nowhere to be seen.

On a visit in late June, when the sun was intense, I wore a shade hat made from bands of grosgrain ribbon. It caught Carlo's eye, and he insisted that I should sit for a portrait. When I demurred, he assured me that it would be completed in a single afternoon. Unrattled by the cluckings of his protective housekeeper—"But Maestro, you will be late for the Senate!"—he set up his easel and prepared his palette.

I observed him as he worked with deliberation, only his eyes, beneath the overhang of his brow, darted back and forth rapidly. And, just like the proverbial tortoise who won the race against the hasty hare, Carlo Levi was confident that his steady pace would accomplish his purpose in the time allotted.

When he laid aside his palette and put down his brushes, he declared,

"I think that I have achieved an excellent likeness. I will keep this one for my personal collection. It will remind me of the good times we have had together."

My husband and I crept around the easel; like criminals about to learn the verdict, we dreaded the confrontation with our own images.

The canvas presented two figures posed before the window framing the familiar patch of bamboo woods dappled by impressionistic sunlight: a dashing Sicilian brigand and someone wearing a striped garden hat, but under its protective, modish brim, I recognized the deep-set coal eyes, the gaunt cheeks of the peasant from Lucania.

Carlo Levi is dead. Is there ever enough time to know another? Through his painting he revealed a contradictory self: a Romantic possessed by obsession—subjective, mysterious, blind, its object, a Godforsaken hamlet with an abandoned population. He never returned to Lucania; his vision remained intact. It endures on the pages of a book.

As for me, I continue to miss Carlo Levi's presence in Rome. These days, I no longer enter the Medici Woods; the Piazza del Popolo is as far as I go.

Chapter Twelve

THE AMERICANS

"Grandfathers—A Memoir," by Christopher Clausen, appeared in *Commentary* in April 1993. It is a thoughtful, personal essay on the costs of immigration—and specifically on Clausen's two immigrant grandfathers, each from a wholly different background and of a wholly different ethnicity. With neither undue blame nor idealization, Clausen, who teaches English literature at Pennsylvania State University, sketches the lives of his two forebears and comes to the conclusion that "it is rarely clear in the end who has been conquered more thoroughly, the immigrant or the new country." He sees now that "the ability to pass at will for a native—the perennial dream of the immigrant—may exact a bitter price from its possessor."

This timely message was overpowered for me, reading Clausen's essay, by an unexpected jolt as memory stirred. And just like someone fishing with a slack line who feels a tug, I raised my catch—a name from the past, out of the obliterating waters of the years.

One of Christopher Clausen's grandfathers, his mother's father, was M.E. Ravage, a Romanian Jew (born Marcus Eli Revici) who made his way to America as a sixteen-year-old boy in 1900 and in an astoundingly brief period of time forged a career as a successful free-lance writer and journalist. This same M.E. Ravage, the author of *An American in the Making: The Life Story of an Immigrant*, was still something of a lion when his daughter, Suzanne, and I became childhood friends and classmates ten years after the book was published in 1917. Now, as I peer backward in an attempt to distinguish the father's features, it is my friend's face that I see instead: hair as black as a gypsy's, serious, intelligent, dark glowing eyes, a long, firm, unchildlike jaw, a head overlarge for her slight body. My obstructed view of her father is formed by the recall of my mother's admiring expression at the mention of his name.

Childhood memories consist of disassociated tableaux separated by stretches of blankness. So now, when I reflect upon the Ravages, with the irrational clarity of a dream, I see that far-off person—myself, a child—staring out our dining-room window, across Park Avenue, where the view of a rosy brick building insists upon intruding on my vision. I knew that it was a girls' school because of a puzzling experience connected with it, and also because at regular hours of the day I could watch apparently unattached, agitating arms and hands maintaining a basketball aloft in a gymnasium on the top floor, at eye level to our apartment. Just like the limbs of trees, divorced from their trunks, these female appendages waved and tossed in the wind-still enclosure. Again and again I was drawn to that window, and I longed as on a magic carpet to fly across the narrow space dividing me from the players, while at other times I had an impulse to pull down the shades, to block out those gesticulating branches of a human forest forever.

When I was about five years old, my mother and I passed through the white, pseudo-colonial door of this academy. We were ushered into a parlor furnished with stiff settees, the floor paved in discreet black-and-white checkerboard linoleum; a grandfather clock in a corner ticked away the moments, politely. Do I remember a maid in a frilly apron, carrying a feather duster, or is she only fancy's butterfly, trapped in astigmatic memory? My mother and I sat, side by side. I am not certain that at that early age I took notice of her ethereal beauty; gradually, as I grew up, and now, two generations later, I marvel at her fair, angelic face, the gentle harmony of her features, the chiseled perfection of bones barely covered by the transparency of her skin just as her nervous temperament and intellectual superiority could hardly be concealed behind the bland amenities required by the bourgeois society to which she belonged. At last the headmistress, discreet and cool as the parlor where we waited, arrived. Her eyes, however, were probing, making me feel as though I were standing naked before a doctor. She and my mother conversed in quiet tones, and I was, largely, overlooked. Occasionally, a stray phrase from the headmistress came my way: ". . . intelligent, but immature . . . perhaps happier in a different type of school . . . we regret, but I am certain you will understand. . . ." On me the words had no particular impact, but as we prepared to leave my mother's face arrested me, blanched and shaken, like someone who has learned of an accident, shocking though foretold.

There was no mention, then or ever, of this incident. Its outcome, however, was my enrollment in a very different school, "semi-private" with "democratic ideals." That somber edifice, occupying an entire block across town on upper Broadway, still stands, but it has been put to other use. Then, it reminded me of an orphanage, and seemed miles away from home. The student body of both sexes came from various economic levels, national and ethnic backgrounds. But first and foremost, we were all

Americans. When we sang the national anthem, our pride was shared, and the "Stars and Stripes" in every classroom was communal property.

Yet, upon looking around, an outlander might well have asked, What is an American? I, for one, felt unworthy of citizenship when I was driven to school in the family limousine, and I persuaded Patrick, our Irish chauffeur who cared for me like a nanny, to let me out before we reached the ponderous black iron portals. If I looked back, I would be sure to see Patrick's familiar stout form, like a faithful bull watchdog standing on the sidewalk until I was safely swallowed up inside. I accelerated my steps.

About the school, I remember best its formidable plant: the maze of long corridors smelling of brass polish, disinfectant, chalk dust, and stale gravy from the cafeteria; our classrooms, a field of small, scarred desks clamped to the floor; bells that shrilled at intervals until, with the final one, the students stampeded, pushing and shoving toward the exit. There, a plaster reproduction of the Venus of Milo stood guard: Armless, with empty eye sockets, she was the first to greet us in the morning, the last to bid us goodbye until tomorrow.

In the vast impersonality of this institution, I found Suzanne, my friend. On weekends, we enjoyed playing at my home or at the Ravages' apartment on Morningside Drive near Columbia University. I liked her pretty brunette mother, who spoke English with a French accent. But her Frenchness was merely decorative, and her Catholicism had withered away like a vestigial organ; she, too, was an American. I saw Suzanne's father rarely. But when he and his wife were guests at dinner, even then I felt him to be strange, in the midst of our own hermetic German-Jewish society.

• • •

Now, I realize he was a relatively new arrival, an East European Jew, and that we feared lest we be identified with Yiddish-speaking people who held to their traditional religion and customs. (My family and their friends would have been surprised to know that the sons and daughters of those very immigrants would soon form the intellectual center of New York City.) Four generations in the United States and the acquisition of wealth had, for the most part, made my family assimilationists. My father's forebears, who liked to think of themselves as German, burghers, inheritors of the Enlightenment, rather than Jews, had handed down a tradition of agnosticism which, by the time it reached my father, had been firmed into atheism, as strict as dogma. Accordingly, in my childhood, a scrupulous avoidance of any knowledge of Jewish roots was the accepted order of my upbringing.

But M.E. Ravage was an exception among his kind, and as such we awarded him welcome and respect. From the remove of the present day, I can still find the position on our library shelf of his autobiography, *An American in the Making*, among such disparate writers as Mark Twain, George Bernard Shaw, Jane Austen, George Meredith, Thomas Carlyle, and Edith Wharton. It was a brave handbook for the "melting pot": It told of his beginnings in a Romanian ghetto, his emigration alone at sixteen, and his rapid rise from sweatshop worker to successful journalist and biographer. Like my parents, he believed in intermarriage, and he had a Christian wife.

Many of our group, resembling honey bees inside a well-appointed hive, were awaiting the season for a general dispersion into and within Western society, innocent, unaware of what the near future held in store for Jews. Their anxiety went no further than the possibility of social exclusion. That topic was avoided in my home, but like a shadow it followed, mutely, the uncertain steps of my growing up.

M.E. Ravage's career as a New York City journalist specializing in European affairs caused him in due course to move with his family to Paris, and my friendship with Suzanne ended then, except for a brief postscript.

One summer, a year after her departure, while traveling abroad, we contacted the Ravages. The reunion took place in the Tuileries Gardens. I was stunned to find that my American friend had turned into a proper Parisian girl, no different from all the others calling out in their games in glib, idiomatic French, at home along the historic paths of the Gardens bordered by statues in the stippled, venerable shade cast by ancient trees. Even the clouds appeared foreign, more massive, pregnant with impending rain showers, in contrast to the fleecy lambs that floated above sunny Central Park. In the lives of children, in inverse ratio to their ages, a year may be as long as a lifetime, and at that last meeting, Suzanne and I had little to say to one another.

But now, having read "Grandfathers—A Memoir," I wrote Christopher Clausen to ask the whereabouts of his mother. It seemed impossible that this middle-aged man could be the son of my friend. I saw her as a nine-year-old shouldering a hoop and waving as we parted in the Tuileries Gardens.

My subsequent letter to Suzanne elicited a prompt response, postmarked Berkeley, California. In a few lines she sketched her uprooted youth in France, her return to the United States for college, marriage on the verge of World War II, the birth of four sons, reared, unlike her, on American soil, her life in the academy. We exchanged, also, some reminders of our briefly shared past: "Do you remember the white statue of the blind, armless goddess standing behind the door of our school?" I asked.

She wrote: "I can still see your brother's marvelous electric train." Our memories did not coincide. Recovery of the past is a lonely pursuit.

Recently, indeed, I received the sad news of the death of Suzanne Ravage Clausen. I had hoped, somehow, that we might meet again. But, despite that unexpected tug on the slackened line of memory, the "once upon a time" of the past can no longer be.

Christopher Clausen concludes his memoir with an account of a visit he paid in the early 1960's to his Jewish grandfather, then living in shabby lodgings in Paris. He was an old man, a failure, isolated (divorced from his first wife, remarried and widowed), without roots, an alien, a fake-American in France.

For me, his features are still hiding behind his daughter's face. But, just like a main character in a play who never is seen on stage, he is pivotal to the plot. I have added a fantasy to Christopher Clausen's account. The year is somewhat later. A student mob is congregated on the tidy grounds of some unnamed university campus. They are proclaiming, self-righteously, the rules of racial and ethnic separatism. I recognize the head, in effigy, of M.E. Ravage, apostle of assimilation, mounted on a pike.

Chapter Thirteen

TWO GOTHIC PROFILES

The tall imposing figures of T. S. Eliot and Pierre Teilhard de Chardin are linked in my mind, their profiles, both with high bony noses like church buttresses, are etched into the future.

When I was at college Eliot was the poet above all others. Inside the mock Tudor campus buildings we sat in informal groups as our Marxist professors taught us from several bibles: *Das Kapital, Man's Fate; The Waste Land,* and *The Hollow Men.* Pseudo-leftists, uniformly dressed in pastel Brooks Brothers sweaters, fake pearl necklaces, and rubber-soled saddle shoes, we all absorbed the poems line by line, convinced that *April is the cruellest month* or *This is the way the world ends/Not with a bang but a whimper* were announcements of the fall of capitalist society. We were molded by our teachers from Monday to Friday. They pointed out to us with astonishing cheerfulness the approaching apocalypse, when they were not too busy listening to our private psychic problems. But on the weekend we returned to our bourgeois existences unaware that our minds were as piebald as our saddle shoes.

My interest in Eliot's poetry was revived by a reading he gave at the Y.M.H.A. in New York. The auditorium was filled to capacity: adolescent students of literature, writers, editors, critics, and fringe colleagues. They appeared eager but somewhat dusty, as though they had dwelt too long among dark library shelves. Sitting near us, two girls in blue jeans and striped T-shirts were vigorously chewing gum. Between snaps and clicks, one of them was saying, "It's not that I care about his poetry, I just want to get a look at him before he dies." This was cold reverence. But was it after all so different from my own image of him? I had not returned to Eliot since my college days but now that my husband had become his publisher I was eager to see the great man in the flesh. Tonight he was to read *The Waste Land*, the manifesto of my student days. He walked slowly from the dark wings across the lighted stage to the lectern. He was tall and angular as a Gothic cathedral, with that prominent nose, his eyes blinking in the sudden glare as sunken and lusterless as burned-out craters. His voice had organ tones, and soon the particulars of the man were lost in the poem itself: The agonized cries of the damned, the bereaved, the sage gazing too deeply into the abyss were interspersed by inane Cockney dialogue, crickets chirping in a graveyard. The political prophecy once disclosed to me by academic mentors was displaced by a vast lament, personal yet universal, more intelligible yet less explicit than the poem I had studied, all footnotes drowned in Eliot's resonant voice.

> Phlebas the Phoenician, a fortnight dead,
> Forgot the cry of gulls, and the deep sea swell
> And the profit and loss.
>   A current under sea
> Picked his bones in whispers. As he rose and fell
> He passed the stages of his age and youth
> Entering the whirlpool.
>   Gentile or Jew
> O you who turn the wheel and look to windward,
> Consider Phlebas, who was once handsome and tall as
>   you.

Later I read for the first time *Four Quartets* and *Ash Wednesday* and discovered the poet of formal religious quietude. The revolutionary spokesman for the "new generation" no longer existed, if he ever had. This grave voice was heard out of a timeless, unending metaphysical present.

During a visit to New York Eliot was staying with his friend and editor, Robert Giroux. As my husband and I entered Giroux's bachelor flat, my first impression of Eliot was again of size. The large, gray, burned-out crater eyes looked surprisingly mild behind his glasses. He was pale; his features had a grandeur that made Giroux look rosy and round beside him. It would not have startled me if Eliot's natural voice had been a clap of thunder. Instead, he spoke with a clipped British accent about the difficulty of obtaining hotel accommodations in the Virgin Islands and about the spring climate in New York City.

"Bob and I sat in the sun in Central Park this afternoon," he said.

"Tom enjoyed watching the children playing," added Giroux, handing around the drinks and appetizers. Although the room still looked overcrowded, Eliot no longer seemed to be the cause. He sat ensconced on a black horsehair sofa, twirling his gold swizzle stick, a gift from an admirer, as he watched the champagne bubbles in his glass with the same expression of passive interest that I imagined he had shown while observing the children at play in the park.

We were going to the theater to see *My Fair Lady* because Cathleen Nesbitt was acting in it and she had starred in Eliot's *The Cocktail Party*. In the taxi there was a discussion as to whether he should go backstage to present his compliments before or after the performance. He was as nervous as any stagedoor Johnny. Bob Giroux listened, advised, encouraged, and with his help the decision was finally taken. He went afterward.

As my turmoil at being with Eliot subsided, I observed with incredulity his mounting excitement, very much as mine had been at the prospect of meeting him.

After the theater we returned to Bob's apartment for a nightcap. The three men talked publishing, Eliot as senior member of Faber and Faber, the English firm. Now I saw him from a new angle: the London man of affairs. It was easy to picture him wearing the regulation bowler hat and chamois vest of the toiler in the City. My husband mentioned a volume of Turgenev reminiscences, never translated into English, that he was about to publish. I watched Eliot take a small pad from his pocket and scribble some notes. His long bony fingers handled the scrap of paper with dexterity, as though he were taking an order. The evening wore on and I managed to smother several yawns, feeling resentful that the T. S. Eliot I had looked forward to meeting had been so effectively concealed.

It was not until the next day that my husband realized that he had unwittingly presented Faber with an editorial acquisition, the unpublished reminiscences of Turgenev. And it was years and several meetings later before I was reconciled to the triviality of my Eliot encounters. I now believe that the vulnerable poet took refuge in the soothing hum of social chit-chat and shop talk just as crustaceans find protection inside the stuffy dark of a shell.

These days I read T. S. Eliot's poetry with increasing awe, but my image of him has become indistinct, as when the silvery disk of an autumnal sun is veiled by passing clouds in formations that imitate various earth species indigenous to us below.

I have no conviction that the man I remember now is the same as the once famous Jesuit philosopher, author of *The Human Phenomenon* and other books, creator of a system of thought whose purpose is the reconciliation of his two passionate loyalties: enduring Mother Church and that upstart ruler Science.

My first view of him antedates World War II. He was brought to our house one summer day by my cousin Rhoda, whose relationship with him, growing closer with the years, was to be my connection. They had met on a geological expedition some time before; now he was passing through the United States on his way to Peking for further paleontological work, a field in which he had already made important discoveries. He was in his late fifties, a tall aristocratic man in severe clerical black and white. His craggy head allowed one to divine the fine bones of his skull. His nose, high-bridged and aquiline, was reminiscent of Voltaire's. This Jesuit priest on his way to distant lands seemed to have no part in my life and I took note of him abstractly, the way one records the features of a passing landscape—vivid, seen in detail for an instant before disappearing forever around a bend in the road.

Yet I was destined to meet Teilhard de Chardin again and often. Through the intricate design of chance, this French priest, after having been interned in China during the war years, was to make New York City his adopted home. And Rhoda, whose path had crossed his in Tibet, was to be his mainstay in exile for as long as he lived. He would be working for a science foundation here because the Catholic Church wanted him out of France, fearing his heretical philosophy that had already found a handful of ardent followers within the Order. But none of us was especially concerned with his ideas; we came to take him for granted as a type of benign and unobtrusive elderly uncle.

The album opens with a snapshot of him seated at the family board at one of the Sunday luncheon rituals at my father's apartment. My father, a recent widower, would gather stray relatives and friends for interminable midday feasts that left us drowsy and stuffed. I see a typical grouping around the enlarged table covered in white damask, where the gold and white English china and cut crystal glasses, used only for evening galas in my mother's day, were now squandered in bachelor negligence throughout the numerous courses of the midday meal. The guests might include Aunt Helen (a relative by appointment rather than consanguinity), my mother's lifelong friend—an ex-beauty with faded rose petal skin, porcelain-blue eyes, a disdainful mouth, and a frizzy *belle époque* bang. She was accompanied by her spinster daughter, who looked like a governess but preserved in regard to her mother the obedient and furtive attitude of a timid child. The family doctor came next, an early Hitler refugee, square and blond with a Heidelberg dueling scar marring his lower lip. He looked most natural when sampling beer, the product of my family's business. Also included was Estelle Leibling, a vivacious friend of my father's, a well-known singing coach who had launched many Metropolitan Opera stars and looked like a retired performer herself; my husband, my brother and his current wife, the motion picture actress Linda Darnell. I see her in full opulent color, with wide rich brown eyes and flowing dark hair; having just arisen she was wearing a negligee that revealed a broad expanse of snowy white chest and the deep cleavage of her bosom like an alpine ravine. She would be sipping genteelly from a tall glass (pure gin), while waiting for a long-distance call from Athens, Rome, or Istanbul concerning a film. Nestled in the capacious sculptured hollow between her neck and shoulder, the camera has caught her pet marmoset, as meager and mangy as his mistress is voluptuous and smooth. He seems to be surveying the assembled guests with fearful disapproving eyes.

Father Teilhard de Chardin might be found next to this exotic pair with the ballast of Rhoda on his other side. But habit, that strongest of sedatives, allowed him to accept them as well as the other guests, just as we grew accustomed to him as merely another member of the group. I no longer examined him with the interested scrutiny of our first meeting. His long black-clothed frame and his white clerical collar were as much a part of the scene as the colorful Chinese screen that had always stood, for no apparent reason, at right angles to the swinging pantry door that divided the dining room from the nether regions in my parents' home. As regularly as the striking of a grandfather's clock, before the demitasses had been served, Father Teilhard would rise from the table and disappear into my father's bedroom for his afternoon nap. Now I understand how his inflexible routine steadied him in the intricate juggling of his philosophic thought and comforted him in the exile against the loss of native land, his Jesuit dwelling in the rue Monsieur in Paris, and the far-flung field trips that he had grown too old to pursue.

In retrospect unbelievable, though natural enough at the time, were my Wednesday afternoon walks in Central Park with Father Teilhard de Chardin. Rhoda had the idea that it would be calming for him and useful for us for him to give us French conversation lessons, so with our tutor between us we would dawdle over the paths, breaking into English whenever we were too lazy to search for the correct word in French. How incongruous these outings appear now, as wasteful as using a priceless Han vase for a common cooking pot.

On fine afternoons we would go to the Zoo for tea. Here on the terrace, surrounded by cages, inhaling the stale pungent odor of captive animals, we would watch the seals, sleek as black silk thread flicking under and over the waters of their mini-ocean. Their hoarse calls were both threatening and forlorn. I have always disliked zoos, but it amused Father Teilhard to see the baboons pacing their prison cells, scratching, defecating, plucking amorously at one another. He regarded this scatological exhibition in much the same way as he saw *les noirs* in South Africa or the Untouchables in India, without compassion, as a scientist. "But one must take the long view. . . ," he would remonstrate. Focusing on the details of here and now was not for him. His deep keen eyes seemed to be approaching the universe in vast evolutionary stretches of time invisible to the rest of us.

One afternoon as we were rising to leave the cafeteria, Father Teilhard dropped the breviary he was carrying and a small card fluttered out and landed on the cement at our feet. It was a picture of Jesus in crude color, like the one I used to examine in the maid's room in my childhood, flanked on her bureau by a faded palm and her rosary. The same mild effeminate face was framed by the spiky gold halo and the plump rosy heart was depicted on the outside like a weeping valentine. As Father Teilhard reached down to retrieve it, our eyes met and a dark flush spread over his face. I wonder, was that flush a symptom of the schism in his mind where the remote philosopher-scientist and the faithful Catholic were constantly seeking accord?

Our country house in Westchester was always pleasing to Father Teilhard de Chardin. He claimed that it reminded him of the home of his childhood, but I could never understand in what way the suburbs of New York City could resemble his ancestral acres in the austere mountains of Auvergne. His birthplace and his large, fanatically religious family, left forever when he entered the priesthood at seventeen, seemed very far away from our casual house and sunny garden, close to encroaching thruways and the noisy intrusion of the county airport. At twilight on summer evenings when we sat outside after dinner, he would gaze at our sprawling roof and the giant pincushions of box hedge in the garden with the relaxed satisfaction of a returned traveler. On these visits to Sarosca Farm he would shed his black suit and clerical collar for a polo shirt and slacks, which he wore with a shade of shy vanity that reminded me of myself putting on my first long evening dress.

Sometime, when my husband and I pass a gas station, Esso, Texaco, or Mobil, its pumps like robots lining the route, we enjoy reminiscing about him and the rides we all used to take through the green, shady countryside. Rhoda, a tourist in reverse, would point out the sights of interest. "Look, Pierre," she would exclaim, "over there is a real American gas station!" And he would absent-mindedly answer, "*Très gentil*," a phrase he often used to describe a person or a place, with that far-off expression in his intense eyes geared only to the "long view."

Father Teilhard was accepting of people and like T. S. Eliot enjoyed the warmth of their proximity, but he was no shepherd and he had no wish for a flock. He was engaged in the solitary battle of the mind and at Sarosca Farm he spent part of each day writing in the guest room, conventional with its leftover, unread novels and ruffled dressing table. His philosophical writings were banned by the Church and they were unread by us too, for we remained strangely incurious about his work. Once, when he was visiting us on the eve of a trip to South America, where he was to attend a scientific conference, the travel bureau called to inquire if he would say Mass on shipboard. When he picked up the telephone his voice sounded unusually harsh, and the flush I had noticed at the zoo as he bent to retrieve the picture of Jesus spread over his features again: "I would rather not say Mass. I am very sorry." Later Rhoda persuaded him to change his mind, which he did, I suspect, more to please her than from any priestly sense of duty.

Season after season, for six years, Father Teilhard de Chardin was with us like a kindly relative, and I saw him only once stripped of the familiar. It was a bleak and windy day, fall or early spring, I no longer remember. The old elm at the end of the garden was bare, its black branches gesticulating wildly in the gale. In the sky, clouds were churning. Through the glass of the French doors, frail protection against the onslaught, suddenly I saw a tall figure, black coattails flapping, a supernatural appari- tion with an open prayer book held in long Gothic hands—a pious scarecrow circling the house. It was a moment before I identified Father Teilhard de Chardin, and then, swiftly as though I had been eavesdropping, before he should notice me I moved to another part of the house.

One other incident has since appeared significant. We were lunching at our country club; it was off season and, stripped of its outdoor uses, the monster clubhouse, like a resort hotel from the twenties, was a blot on the landscape. Rhoda, Pierre, my husband and I were seated at a table near a window overlooking the golf course, dotted sparsely with a few hardy players muffled up against the cold. The big dining hall was overheated and over-decorated with gilded columns and wainscoting. The club membership includes many Irish Catholics, and this day saw the usual complement of fat, well-fed priests. Father Teilhard, though wearing the same habit, looked a breed apart, with his narrow head, his penetrating eyes, and his cultivated, slightly French accent. He was like a princely guest in the plush and gold drawing room of the nouveaux riches. Perhaps moved by his unselfconscious superiority, I had an unusual impulse to talk to him about his writing. "How do you have the patience to go on?" I asked. "The Church has muzzled you. Will you ever be published if you remain a part of it?" I had heard from Rhoda about his endless and unavailing appeals to the Vatican.

"It is no matter," Father Teilhard answered. "My thought is for the Church. Outside, I could no longer serve it. I am confident that Catholicism will go my way. If I am instrumental, good; if not, I am content to be a drop in the sea. The essential is that what I believe will prevail in the end."

He looked directly at me, then down at his neglected fruit cup and abruptly changed the subject, but not before I had caught a spark illuminating something rare in our midst.

Immediately following his death in the fifties his works were released by the Church and acclaimed by the world. But, in another later swing of the pendulum, religion (all sects) having taken on renewed strength and science having lost some of its impetus, Teilhard de Chardin's attempt at the fusion of his two dedications was no longer vital. Along the streets of New York, in book store windows his works and the display photograph of his bony face that resembled Voltaire's are long gone.

"Did you really know him?" people used to ask. Now they say ". . . but who was he?"

In protest against inconstant fame, in memory of Pierre Teilhard de Chardin, I place my scraps of recollection before the altar remains of a skeletal cathedral.

Chapter Fourteen

ACROSS THE TIBER

"My new address is 45 Lungo Tevere della Vittoria," said Alberto Moravia, the Italian novelist. Then, as further information, he added, "The street has many workers."

My husband (Moravia's American publisher) and I decided to make the visit on foot. As we approached the river, the Castel Sant'-Angelo fortress (originally Hadrian's tomb) rose before us, its circular wedding cake form posing ponderously for a picture postcard of itself. The Tiber bisects Rome, but unlike the Seine, it does not seem to be integrated into the life of the city. It is said that in bygone times, the sluggish, muddy, watery serpent's breath was believed to carry malaria. After crossing the Sant'-Angelo Bridge, we found ourselves on a street lined with new, low apartment houses, identical in their middle-class conformity. I had not known before that such ordinariness existed in the center of Rome; perhaps we had taken a wrong turn, and I searched in vain for the landmark workers, the road construction mentioned by Moravia. However, the street sign read Lungo Tevere della Vittoria—and here was number 45. We had arrived at our destination.

The glass and chromium lift carried us to the top floor, where Moravia waited. Under the surgical glare of a skylight, his tan polished skin, topaz eyes, square jaw, jutting nose, and his virtually lipless mouth that resembled the long, narrow slash of a saber wound, were revealed unsparingly. He greeted us with cordiality, but his mode of speech was clipped, ironic. In his sixties, he was still fit, hard, and spare as an athlete. But as he led the way inside, I was shocked anew by his limp, profound as a series of mocking bows. He managed this handicap (the result of a childhood illness) with bravura, but just as a skilled equestrian controls an evil steed, Moravia and his crippling were locked in perpetual combat.

The guests, the usual complement of left-wing intellectuals who flourished in the 1960s and '70s, were strewn over the deep upholstery of the sofas and armchairs in Moravia's living room. They brought to mind the street-smart army of cats congregated in a passage between the Piazza Novona, a spacious oval outdoor salon, hosted by Bernini's sea gods towering over their fountain basins, and the Piazza del Campo's market that provided ample meals for the feline population.

Alberto Moravia, like his companions, was a socialist; his early and continuing fame had made him something of a leader, an indispensable member of the group that met at Rosati's Café in the Piazza del Popolo. But his wealthy bourgeois background set him apart. For him, this legacy, like his lameness, was a foe that must be subdued, daily, through his writings and his political beliefs.

"Come, look at my view," he said, and we moved to the window.

The unobstructed vista revealed a long stretch of river; on the opposite shore one could see only some public tennis courts and institutional buildings. But, by craning my neck, I caught sight of St. Peter's dome, its stately, rotund dominance visible, it seems, everywhere, asserting the spell that is Rome.

I praised the panorama as much as possible, and then, for no apparent reason, I asked, "Where are the workers you spoke of?"

"You can see one strolling along the embankment," he answered.

A young woman in a tight miniskirt, wearing spike-heeled shoes, black lace stockings, and carrying a green plastic bag, was walking back and forth among hurrying pedestrians.

"They come out in numbers only at night," said Moravia.

He watched her greedily, as though he were absorbing the living being in order to prove the veracity of his best-selling novel, *Woman of Rome*. This first-person narrative is told by a prostitute, a heroine without glamour, a soldier in a losing battle; a sexual hedonist, despite her profession, armored in innate goodness. Unlike Flaubert's Emma Bovary, the product of detached realism, Adriana is born from Moravia's socialist imagination.

When we rejoined the others, they were deep in argument on a topic popular that season in Rome. A millionaire publisher had been killed by a bomb in suspected confrontation with a cabal of neo-Fascists. The disputers were divided into two camps: those claiming that the radical amateur activist had blown himself up by accident, due to his clumsiness and lack of experience, while others insisted that he had been murdered by the enemy. But everyone was united in eulogy extending beyond graveside to the salons, trattorias, editorial pages of liberal newspapers, and lecture halls of the city.

The door opened; and just like a draft of fresh air that disperses the dry leaves of autumn, Dacia Maraini, the young mistress and literary protégée of Moravia, entered the room, accompanied by a large, shaggy hunting dog. The debate of the savants faltered, and Moravia exclaimed,

"Ah! Here she is, finally. Dacia has been spending a few days at my house in the country."

Indeed, her short blond curls were still damp from swimming in the sea, and her pert, snub-nosed face rosy after a recent gallop along the sand. She wore a boy's shirt, open at the throat, and her strong legs were defined in jodhpurs.

"I'm famished," she said. "Let's eat."

At last we could take our places around the dining table, and I noticed, for the first time, that Dacia and I were the only women present. As soon as we were seated, Moravia announced, with paternal boastfulness,

"I am certain that all of you have read the excellent reviews Dacia has received for her new novel."

Dacia's rosy face remained impassive, but her sullen silence (broken only when addressed directly) indicated boredom, rather than the shyness of an ingenue among veteran professionals, an acolyte in the presence of cardinals and bishops, the elite of a literary Vatican.

I observed our host. His table manners reminded me of his mode of speech; the food disappearing between his narrow, saber-slash lips in impatient gulps, while he evinced no ray of gourmand enjoyment. As the maid passed the tall, noble roast on a silver platter, the smell of rich gravy transported me back to my father's Sunday family luncheons. But, as in a dream in which the familiar turns strange and one blunders in quest of the past, my assorted relatives, long dead, had become these foreigners, the Italian guests of Alberto Moravia. I wondered—was Moravia aware that this ritual meal marked him as a gentleman of the bourgeoisie, as surely as his scorn for this class from which he had sprung qualified him as a respected member of the Italian left wing?

Moravia achieved immediate renown for his first novel, *The Time of Indifference*, written when he was in his early twenties. While *Woman of Rome*, a work from his maturity, is a bitter serenade to the proletariat, *The Time of Indifference* pronounces a curse upon the bourgeoisie. The story revolves around one family: mother, daughter, son, and a vastly wealthy businessman, the lover of both the mother and daughter. Merumici helps to support the household in luxury and his money has made him master. Michele (a self-portrait?), the son, contemplates the murder of this diabolical protector. But his inertia, more than the enormity of the crime, arrests him as he wanders the streets plotting the act. He pauses in front of a perfume shop whose show window is piled high with a pyramid of expensive colored soaps. A cardboard dummy built on human scale is passing a razor blade backwards and forwards. The imbecile figure was used "to display the quality of the razor . . . but Michele is looking at himself, his own sincerity—and what caught his eye, was not the smiling dummy, but the blade itself . . . the essential thing is that it shaves . . ." Action, any action, is preferable to indifference, he tells himself, as he anticipates the future. He, his sister, Carla, and the Signora, strangling on material things, will continue their useless existence: shopping, going out to afternoon tea, balls and convening regularly at mealtime in mute hostility to one another, unable to escape the grasp of Signor Merumici. *The Time of Indifference* is a young man's novel, but the theme of self-hatred may be found, often, in later works.

Back in the living room, after the espresso cups had been cleared from the coffee table, Moravia brought out an album of photographs taken on a recent safari he and Dacia had made to

South Africa. Picture after picture showed them surrounded by natives.

"You can have no idea of the dignity of these people," Moravia said.

One snapshot showed Dacia with sophisticated camera equipment slung over her shoulder.

"If we put down our cameras for even one moment, they were stolen," Moravia continued, seemingly oblivious to this negation of the "noble savage."

But my attention was caught elsewhere. The shaggy hunting dog was stretched out at his master's feet. Without interrupting his account of adventures in Africa, Moravia reached down to pat the animal; as he buried his hand in the thick fur, his topaz eyes softened and seemed to melt. And, just as one may experience a brief electric shock in contacting a light switch in a cold room, I imagined that I felt the surprisingly tender touch of Moravia's hand upon my own shoulder.

Evening arrived before the luncheon gathering disbanded, but I was certain that the comrades would be meeting again at the Café Rosati, to talk into the small hours of the morning.

Alberto Moravia survived into his eighties, his writing continued prolific, highly praised and much read. His body remained hard, and his prominent nose and chin jutted more aggressively in old age. A mutual friend described his funeral. To honor more than half a century of fame in Italy, his casket was placed on public view on the steps of the Campidoglio in the shadow of the equestrian statue of Marcus Aurelius. The crowds, numerous as city pigeons, clustered to pay homage to the author. I was told that he suffered no lingering illness, but had been extinguished suddenly, at home, while shaving. Yet my own fantasy picture of his end persists: I see Moravia, but he is not alone. A barber, a rough member of the working people, stands over him, manipulating the sharp edge of a razor. Although a mask covers the lower part of the face of this tonsorial apparition, his eyes are revealed, topaz-golden, pilfered from Moravia, who lies on the floor of his bathroom, dead, a green brocade dressing gown his shroud.

Chapter Fifteen

A VOICE FROM THE FIRST GENERATION

Bernard Malamud and his wife, Ann, dined with us on an evening in 1986, when, in his words, "winter was on its last legs." On the surface, the gathering resembled many others we had shared, dating back thirty years. During that time there were also readings by Malamud of his work in progress at his home on West Seventieth Street, and at an assortment of parties where we met—I can name a whole population of fellow guests—but at this dinner, try as I may, I remember only Bern.

I see his slow, yet unhesitating entrance into our living room. He had been in poor health, but, in his peaceable fashion, Bern was a fighter and neither illness nor his age (seventy-one) had managed to make inroads into his essential, idiosyncratic self. He appeared smaller than before, but the observant intelligence of his brown eyes, behind spectacles, was as unflinching as ever. They spoke for him, as well as his speech (which was slower, now, too). Talking to Bernard Malamud could never be a disappointing experience; at a dining room table or seated, companionably, on a sofa, he has taught me more than any professor on a dais.

I am able to record only a few phrases, out of context, but I hoard them. They are both larger and lesser than when they were uttered. "What do years matter as long as they are not wasted? Each one that comes makes better the bargain," or, "the human being is imperfect . . . the ideal is not . . ." Malamud, the consummate writer of fiction—part teacher, part scholar—was always a striver whose seriousness was tempered by his special brand of wry humor. In one of his most powerful fable-type stories, *The Last Mohican*, the anti-hero, Fidelman, a failed artist, and his ghostly counterpart, the peddler, duel in words, at once comic and sinister.

We often talked about our favorite authors—especially the nineteenth-century Russians, Marcel Proust, and Virginia Woolf. On this evening, sitting next to one another at the table, we seemed to pick up our conversation where we had left off the time before. We were actors taking part in a long run, and I had no intimation that the play was about to close.

After dinner, Malamud rose from his chair, early. "I must go home now," he said. "Tomorrow there will be a long morning of work on my novel."

I followed his cautious step down the stairs. And, with Ann beside him, he disappeared into the street.

At about noon the next day, Bernard Malamud died at his worktable, while fulfilling his resolutions—his last hours, unwasted.

Despite my awareness of his precarious health, the shock was great—and the loss. Many other memories of him have been expunged by the sad, inadvertent drama of that good-bye. But the night of March 1986 is with me. Seated at my right, there is Bern with his cup of tea, as usual. The years have brought a measure of consolation to the recall of the last meeting, at the very end of Bernard Malamud's life I was privileged to find in him no diminution. His wisdom, his humor, his pride, as well as his humility were intact.

Now, when I reread his wonderful stories, I discover him again: the frail, strong man; the secular Jew with his firm code of ethics; his belief in reason—product of the enlightenment, the American Diaspora, master of paradox, who, in his writing, often glanced back ruefully and with some regret, to a mystical past he could no longer espouse.

Bern, I know you hated to be classified as a "Jewish writer." I agree that all categories (black, woman, Jew) are reductive. Yet, if I may venture a paradox, myself, I believe that your spirit, as well as the engaging cadence of your prose, are, indeed, quintessential first-generation Jewish. And I am grateful. You have given testimony to best of kind—through your writings and in your person.

During my childhood I was unaware of the existence of Ellis Island. And I have never learned the name of the port of entry used by my ancestors, German Jews, who arrived in this country with the wave of immigration of 1848. Yet, today, Ellis Island is a favorite tourist site for the ethnically conscious citizens of New York City who come in flocks to inspect its bare halls in memory of the thousands who passed through at the turn of the century on their way to becoming Americans. But when I was growing up, in the days before the Holocaust, we discarded our history as Jews, and just as people in good health avoid contact with tuberculosis, still insecure, we feared contagion from the new Jewish arrivals from the ghettos of Eastern Europe, uninoculated with the remedies (now outmoded) from the "melting pot."

In the late nineteenth century, the young Alfred Stieglitz, himself a wealthy German Jew, photographed *Steerage* (in my view, a picture more sentimental than moving) from the vantage of first class aboard an ocean liner. In the crowd on the lower, uncovered deck, one might recognize the face of the Russian,

Morris Bober, out of *The Assistant*, a novel by Bernard Malamud. The son of an immigrant, the author used his father as model; a memorial more vital than the preserved stones and halls of Ellis Island.

The action of *The Assistant* is confined to a block in a low-income section of the Bronx, one rung up the ladder from the East Side ghetto. Here, among poor Jews and Gentiles, Morris Bober, a grocer, ekes his meager living. The reader becomes familiar with the cans of soup, cold meats, and three-penny rolls on the shelves; with Morris, one waits for the all-too-infrequent ring of the cash register and one watches Bober's awkward descent from the cramped family apartment upstairs above the shop at dawn, his weary return at night. Though physically weak, the grocer is fortified by his unswerving adherence to the Law. Just as the roof and four walls of a house in his own country are protection for most human beings, for the ghetto Jew of the Diaspora, the Torah and the Talmud constitute an internal home, transportable from one alien land to another. When we meet Morris, he has already evolved from the strict ritual of orthodoxy, but his allegiance to Jewish law remains intact. In an expressive amalgam of Yiddish-American, Morris talks to Frank Alpine, his Italian-Gentile assistant, a reformed tramp and petty criminal.

"This is not important to me if I taste pig or I don't. To some Jews, this is important, but not to me. Nobody will tell me that I am not Jewish because I put in my mouth, once in a while when my tongue is dry, a piece of ham. But they will tell me and I will believe them if I forget the Law. This means do what is right, to be honest, to be good. This means to other people. Our life is hard enough. Why should we hurt someone else? For everybody should be the best, not only for you and me. We ain't animals. This is why we need the Law. This is what a Jew believes."

When Frank answers that other religions have these ideas, but that "Jews suffer so damn much, it seems like they like to suffer—" Morris says,

"If you live you suffer. Some people suffer more, but not because they want. But I think if a Jew don't suffer for the Law, he will suffer for nothing."

Despite the sadness, a continuous river flowing through the book, there is, also, a current of vigorous, ironic humor, indigenous to many Jewish fiction writers, Malamud, especially. Speaking of his hard lot, the grocer has the detachment to query, "How complicated could impossible get?"

Bernard Malamud, a consummate stroyteller, is, as well, a wise, compassionate psychologist who deals with sexual passions, family loyalties and quarrels, envy, hope, fears, and ambitions. He knows about sleazy deals and crimes and he finds lofty generosity where it is least expected. Although Morris Bober is an anti-hero, gentle, seedy, stumbling, his inner dignity, his courageous patience, his patient courage raise him up to warrior without weapons. The characters in the book are various, although Malamud uses a minimum of description; In spare, telling strokes, through dialogue and behavior, his people come alive with all their blemishes and beauty, psychic as well as physical.

Following the grocer's death, the assistant, who has been working for almost no pay to atone for an earlier hold-up of the store, steps symbolically into his employer's shabby shoes in an attempt to resuscitate the failing business, and Frank Alpine continues to be stubbornly in love with the grocer's daughter, in spite of the gulf of race and culture. The relationship is left unresolved, intermarriage remains a question: A viable future for

Jews? or an ancient, unalterable transgression? Malamud offers no utopian solution but the book concludes with a violent act of assimilation in reverse: Frank Alpine, the Christian, has himself circumcised. "After Passover, he became a Jew." With this sentence, the story ends.

The world of the turn-of-the-century Jewish immigrant in New York has vanished; the first generation is going, too, but the voice of Bernard Malamud continues to resonate.

Chapter Sixteen

A MASTER

"You will recognize my house by the sign *Petite Plaisance* and by the fields in front of it," said the writer Marguerite Yourcenar.

Petite Plaisance, the name sounded at once regal and casual and combined with the vision of a sweep of acres. It conjured up in my mind's eye a picture of one of those purportedly small chateaux, resembling the photographs that used to hang in the compartments of the French trains. It would be my first meeting with Madame Yourcenar, and from her books it seemed fitting to find her in a dwelling only slightly less splendid than the palace of a king—a royal retreat like Josephine Bonaparte's Malmaison or the Petit Trianon of Marie-Antoinette— for her writings are aristocratic, self-assured, products of an old culture and scholarship, each book bearing the stamp of a rightful monarch of letters.

But Marguerite Yourcenar (the pen name is an acronym from the original, de Crayencour), born in Brussels of a Belgian mother and French father, no longer lived in Europe. She had been relocated for many years at Mount Desert Island, Maine. So pilgrimage there was thronged with the usual summer weekend travelers to New England. At take-off at Bar Harbor, the local, one-engine propeller plane spluttered and coughed as if to shatter its rickety sides. But, just as an ancient servitor resists retirement and relegation to a nursing home, faced with its inevitable end in the junk yard, the taxi plane rose haltingly off the ground. There was no *post chaise*, nor caparisoned horses to take us to *Petite Plaisance*.

Madame Yourcenar had reserved a room at the best inn at Northeast Harbor, close to where she lived. As I entered the lobby, I felt cool relief from the intense heat outdoors but, at the same time, an amorphous psychic chill. The lobby was welcoming enough, a comfortable American turn-of-the-century period piece. The delectable smell of freshly baked bread drifted from the dining room, lingering after a hearty New England breakfast that was as much a part of the inn, I was to discover, as the repeated story of the great fire in 1889 that had destroyed the whole structure. But it had been rebuilt, a duplicate of the original: Walls painted lemon-yellow, dormer windows, even the obsolete exterior fire escapes, climbing the façade, had been replaced. At the back of the reception room, tall windows opened to a splendid view of the marina, crowded with white sails as burgeoning as lilies. From the wooded hills surrounding the inlet, here and there, a roof, a wall, door, or window—bits and pieces belonging to the spacious homes of the wealthy vacationers from Boston, Providence, Philadelphia, and New York—peeked through the dense green. They seemed to proclaim: This forest belongs to us, our preserve; the ocean is our swimming hole, the marina a nautical playpen.

On the veranda of the hotel, hanging over a bluff open to the gracious scene, lounge chairs were aligned like the statues of Chinese dragons. Each one was preempted by an elderly woman in similar pastel summer attire, though the long white dresses, picture hats, and parasols of Edith Wharton's heroines would have suited better. For the ladies on the porch, the swaying sails must have been melancholy reminders of former days when they, too, had boated and commandeered large households of servants and children of their own. Now, at the inn, they sat on the veranda, useless; gossiping, busy with their knitting and bridge games, waiting the arrival of another meal hour, punctual as the chimes of the grandfather's clock in the lobby.

Following Marguerite Yourcenar's directions, my husband and I walked along the street of her town in search of *Petite Plaisance*. We passed the usual village shops and the modest homes, each with its parsimonious allotment of front lawn. At the end of the road we came to a tall fieldstone wall with an iron grill gate, the entrance to an estate. But the name outside was unknown. Beyond, there was only virgin woods. Puzzled, we retraced our steps, reading each sign with care. In front of a small shingle house, no different from its neighbors, with a stingy square of grass spread before it like a mat, we saw with disbelief, the name: *Petite Plaisance*. We had arrived.

Upon entering, the interior was so obscure that I was able to distinguish our hostess only in silhouette: a massive form moving with measured dignity to greet us. The voice was calm, mannish, the words strongly French accented. She seemed to fill the limited space to brimming, and like a classical structure rising above an overcrowded district, she dwarfed the clutter of furniture. Growing accustomed to the interior twilight, I was now able to discern the pillared cupboard, the claw-footed chairs and tables, gilt trimmed, the heavy, wintry burgundy red-tasseled curtains of an empire, urban, bourgeois decor. As in a dream, I groped for that other place that my imagination had created, more real than this solid setting in which I found myself. But just as someone who falls out of love is confounded when he sees, finally, the real object of his obsession, and relinquishes that other image, I was forced to forgo the aristocratic retreat of my fancy and to accept this stuffy salon on the main street of a New England village.

Marguerite Yourcenar and my husband, her publisher, were discussing the publication of a forthcoming book on the Japanese writer, Mishima. I had leisure to examine her and her appearance, unlike her setting, was not at variance with my expectations. The creator of *Memoirs of Hadrian* looked more imperial Roman than French. Nearing eighty, she remained ageless, her ponderous body denoting power rather than excess. Her head was large, sculptural, the white hair brushed back from a spacious brow. Her features were generous, only the eyes, under heavy brows, were small, of undetermined color, as if the acute intelligence of their glance, like some strong acid, had burned away pigment, leaving only spark and depth.

A miniature gray poodle bounded into the room, interrupting the business discussion. I noted a new tone of tenderness in Marguerite Yourcenar's voice as she said: "This is Trier. He is the latest in a long line of pets. Soon, I will show you my dog cemetery in the garden."

A dog's cemetery! Hadrian's tomb would have been less surprising!

She continued talking about the book in progress. No detail—jacket design, type, the quality of paper—was over-looked. She had strong opinions on everything; her courteous suggestions had been thought through with meticulous care. And yet, there were manuscript pages scattered everywhere, on every inch of space. They seemed to flutter like wings and, at first glance, I feared that something would be lost. However, Yourcenar's serenity reassured me. Other authors might require more outward order, but the prose of Marguerite Yourcenar has the beauty of perfect control: This outward flurry of paper, any domestic disorderliness, could only be apparent.

We sat down to lunch at a small table next to the living room window facing the street, partially hidden by those wine red portieres. And I seemed to hear the sounds of the Paris of the Second Empire issuing from behind their stately folds, the clopping of horseshoes on cobblestones, the cries of street vendors, and the smell of sausage hanging outside a neighboring butcher shop. Most certainly, the meaty smell was not from our frugal meal. A bowl of shiny cranberries, resembling old-fashioned milliner's trim, was placed at the center of the table, flanked by salad greens, Greek olives, and coarse, crusty peasant bread.

"I grow these berries myself," said Marguerite Yourcenar, handing the dish with pride.

I watched her as she ate. Here was no sated emperor, nor was she an ascetic. She tasted the cranberries thoughtfully, as though to extract their very essence. Marguerite Yourcenar was sensual, sentient, a potentate who, having lived through a rich variety of sensory experience, had come to relish the ordinary fruits of the world with a connoisseur's pleasure born of past hedonism now tempered by the mellow autumnal wisdom of age. It was no accident that her remarkable "imaginary" memoir of the Emperor Hadrian was in the works for about thirty years. Often begun, often interrupted by travel, war, love, illness, but still there until the writer's voice merged with that other one, dusty with time, and the completed book seemed more an act of magicianly perpetuity than a contrived memoir. Here at a luncheon table in Maine sat Marguerite Yourcenar, the alchemist who had made this fusion, delecting in her homegrown cranberries, like the aging Emperor himself experimenting with his sophisticated senses. While, to my uneducated palate, the fruit tasted merely bitter.

After lunch, as she had promised, we looked at her

garden, the site of the dog cemetery, at the back of the house. The forest crept around the sunny area, dark and unfathomable, causing the frail blooms to appear valiant and transitory. It would have been easy to miss the graves marked by flat paving stones if she had not pointed them out, while Trier, the current companion, ran about insouciantly among the memorials to his predecessors.

My husband and I stayed until late, talking of many things, mainly about several books planned for the future.

"If time is given me," she added serenely.

Her conversation was detached, her ego requiring neither adulation nor boasting to sustain it. I told her that I had been reading *Archives du Nord*, a memoir-biography that opens with a sketch of Flanders in the age of the caveman. At the advent of the late Middle Ages, Madame Yourcenar is able to weave into her book the histories of members of her father's Flemish-French ancestry (landowners, petty nobility, bourgeoisie), with the somber earth-toned threads of an antique tapestry, here and there, effaced by age. By the nineteenth century, the memoir grows more detailed and personal, but the book concludes with the birth of the author.

She told us that she was considering a sequel to her diptych (the first volume, inversely, begins with her birth and travels back a generation) ". . . but I will stop when I am fifteen," she said. "No one should attempt to write about oneself beyond that age, one becomes self-conscious, the temptation to embellish is too strong—and, after all, is it so important?"

When we left, she accompanied us to the entrance. She had thrown a thin, white wool scarf over her head, protection against the cool Maine evening descending. Now she resembled a monument to the European immigrant. Yet she could not be regarded as an exile. French (the first woman to be admitted to their Academy), Belgian, New England townswoman, world traveler—she was all of these, and none. Her country lay behind her capacious forehead and its wealth in the rich and varied produce of her prose.

At the inn, it was dinner time. The aging widows and divorcées were descending the stairs, gingerly. Some were already sitting in the lounge waiting for the dining room doors to open. They had changed from their day costumes to drooping evening chiffons. And they wore, discreetly, jewels extracted from collections prudently stored in their bank vaults, glittering emblems to remind themselves and one another that they were emeritus, retired from a better lifestyle, reduced in pleasure, perhaps, but not in status. Like a Greek chorus in flowered draperies, earrings, clips, and necklaces, they lamented the passing of youth in falsely chirping voices. As we followed the crowd of fluttering, chatting dowagers into the dining room, I was thankful for that other existence in a saltbox house nearby. I could not help contrasting the old wax-work figures at the inn with that solitary, imperial presence. Was she writing at her desk, surrounded by a storm of manuscript pages? Perhaps she was just sitting in her armchair, musing, with Trier, the last of a succession of favorites, at her feet.

Marguerite Yourcenar has died. Like the Emperor Hadrian, she suffered from vascular disease and, like him, also, I am certain she watched the course of her own end with melancholy, scientific, philosophical interest until, at last, she, too, was able to say to herself: "I am beginning to discern the profile of death." Surprisingly, she bequeathed *Petite Plaisance* to the town as a museum, and she is buried in the local cemetery. I do not believe that many pilgrims will visit her memorials in Mount Desert Island.

Let us look once more at this unassuming house, its obscure history, and the obscure people connected with it. Early, perhaps in the eighteenth century, long ago in the annals of American settlers, a carpenter built its uncomplicated frame and covered it with simple wood shingles that could weather harsh, salt wind. A glazier inserted windowpanes (years later, smothered in deep red drapes, by a French author). Generations of housewives polished, swept, kneaded, scoured, mended, and preserved the clearing against the encroachment of the forest where wildlife roamed and died. The village men were hunters, fishermen, and the lighthouse on the bluff welcomed the mariners when they returned to harbor. The small house was not visible at once, but a candle in the front parlor window at night summoned homewards.

I have chosen to close this memoir with a bow to *Petite Plaisance*: palace of a kind. There could be no better model than Marguerite Yourcenar's inspired serenade to the Château of Chenonceaux:[5]

> A visit to old houses can lead to points of view we did not anticipate.

[5] *"Ah Mon Beau Château," The Dark Brain of Piranesi and Other Essays*, trans. Richard Howard in collaboration with the author (Farrar, Straus & Giroux).

Chapter Seventeen

DEMONS AND SUPERNATURAL PRESENCES

The supernatural has been overtaken largely by the forces of the subconscious. "Good" and "Evil" have become "Sick" and "Well," but I knew, once, a demon. He crossed my path, a slender streak of fire and ice; I shall not see his like again.

There is a certain street corner, a sidewalk café, a special table with a particular view on the Quai Voltaire in Paris that, just as a monument commemorates a patriot, brings back to me the Polish writer, Jerzy Kosinski. Before the hour of our meeting, that location had been no more than an empty stage set, awaiting the appearance of the leading actor.

Paris is divided in two by the Seine, and as you sit at the Café Quai Voltaire, in front of you, across the river, you look at the Right Bank: the dignified government buildings, the Louvre in the formal paths of the Tuileries Gardens, and beyond, the arcades of the Rue de Rivoli. This elegant cityscape is haunted by the shades of the *bel époque*: the *nouveaux riches* on display in their grand *équipages* or strolling among the geometric flower beds in the park, the ladies in long, rustling skirts carrying parasols, the gentlemen, high-hatted, in swallowtail coats. At your back, that maze of streets is the Left Bank, where you might fancy that the priest, whose cassock sweeps the dusty cobblestones, has stepped out of the Middle Ages. Here the ancient houses huddle, shabby and somber, mourning for their aristocratic tenants beheaded in the Revolution. A peoples' market, frequented by students and artists, permeates the atmosphere with the odors of vegetables and fruits. Adjacent to the café, there is a small hotel, where Oscar Wilde languished in inquisitorial banishment. The frontage sleeps; I have seen no guest going in or out, and the filigree balconies resemble the inscriptions on a headstone. To your right, the flow of the Seine leads you towards the sturdy twin towers of Nôtre-Dame, joining the two continents of Paris more surely than the spans of its many bridges. But if you draw close to the cathedral, its bastion contours are obscured in a welter of stone gargoyles—all manner of supernatural shapes—that seem to be saying Right Bank, Left Bank, are one; and evil lurks in cities, the creations of man.

On a fair spring afternoon in the 1960s, my husband and I were resting at the Café Quai Voltaire from one of those long, aimless rambles irresistible to the traveler in Paris. I was content to sit indefinitely at the white-clothed table watching the pedestrians passing by. Suddenly, as though at command from an invisible director, the film blurred, the crowd seemed to go into slow motion, and a single figure emerged, highlighted. When this stranger stopped at our table, I felt no surprise; the encounter had happened before—perhaps, in another existence. It was a déjà vu in the city of déjà vus. Where had I seen that swarthy face with its hawk-like nose, the crest of hair, luxuriant and glossy as a raven's plumage springing from a peak on the low, broad forehead, the heavy black eyebrows, the small pointed ears, that body, thin as a razor blade, moving gracefully, lightly, as though in defiance of gravity? Was he the embodiment of a folk tale: a mischievous demon who stole the souls of pure village maidens and tweaked the noses of pious scholars bowing over their religious tomes? He might be the son of a king, transformed by a magic spell into a gypsy wayfarer. And I felt that, just as lightning splits an unchanging sky, this presence was empowered to disperse the placid, prudent, smug beliefs of the common-sensical quotidian.

Yet he said, only, "How nice to see you. May I sit down?" His accent was faintly foreign, his words, staccato, issuing like ice pellets from his narrow lips.

My husband had known Jerzy Kosinski in New York City, and now he told us that he was about to return there for the publication of his first novel, *The Painted Bird*. The conversation that afternoon was unremarkable, but when he fixed his glance on me with his wide-set black eyes, and commented, "I like your witch's hat," it was as though he were admitting me into a charmed circle. Although I had no idea, then nor now, what this occult order might be, I conserved the black leather hat until it fell apart, its tall crown collapsed, its brim grown shapeless and frayed.

As soon as it was issued, I read *The Painted Bird*, and, for all the time I knew him, Kosinski was defined by this book. It recounts the experience of a six-year-old boy, let loose, alone, in the forest, fleeing the Nazis. He came from a wealthy, upper-middle-class home, privileged with books, toys, a nanny, and cultured parents, but from the first pages the child is presented as a wild gypsy, whose dramatic dark coloring makes him easy prey for his blond, Nordic predators. The narrative tells of his wanderings and his miraculous escapes during the war years. He seeks asylum in huts and farms and, everywhere, he is exposed to murder, rape, sadism, sodomy, incest, and the spells of half-human peasant crones. The small protagonist is wily, agile, and resourceful; he has the courage of those unacquainted with self-pity. A sprite, he manages to survive and terror renders him strong as an army of one. He is oddly detached from the suffering of human beings. His pity is, chiefly, for animals who accept their hideous fates with dumb stoicism. A description of the death of a single cart horse brings tears to the reader's eyes, while the corpses of men and women are cause for nausea and shock. Armed with his "comet," a type of lantern used as seeing eye, stove, body warmer, and amulet, the boy lives, at intervals, in the woods. In winter he glides over the ice with the help of a handmade contraption, part skates, part sail. He binds himself in rags against the cold. In summer, he feels close to the small creatures of the forest, and somehow manages to evade the fangs of the wolves. His rapport with nature is spontaneous, unpoetical, difficult to explain in a pampered city child, but it is never doubted. Magic has its own reasons, unsuspected by the rationale of the psychologist. At the close of the book, at the war's end, the boy is befriended, temporarily adopted by a unit of Russian occupation soldiers, but the dark-painted bird is still isolated from the flock, his loneness is now reinforced by silence, for trauma has made him mute.

The Painted Bird is unique in the literature of the Holocaust, arousing shudders more than empathy. Hell is not to be depicted in humanistic terms. Of course, the tiresome cliché arises: Is it autobiography or fiction? *The Painted Bird* is fantastic as the grotesques in a painting by Hieronymus Bosch, painful as cautery.

This work and a second novel, *Steps*, made Jerzy Kosinski a celebrity. He could be seen at New York City's literary gatherings, still outstanding, as though his fellow writers and acquaintances had cut a swath around him. Urbane, impeccable, he wore smartly tailored, made-to-order suits, pinched here, flared there, to accentuate his swaggering grace. Although his height was average, his glossy black head, with curls clustering around his pointed ears, and his swarthy sardonic face, seemed to top the company. He was difficult to know, and just as a performer is concealed by his roles, Kosinski was elusive through many guises and his tall tales of pursuit, international espionage, and torture. By turn, he had been impoverished, homeless, or rich, with an apartment in every city of Europe complete with a duplicate wardrobe so that he could take off free of baggage at a moment's notice. He played polo and skied with the jet set; hob-nobbed, disguised as a professor, with academics in secluded quadrangles; wandered, alone, at dawn, through slum streets and along docksides festering with vice.

He described to me several versions of his whirlwind courtship of the young widow of a millionaire Pittsburgh industrialist. The contact had been made soon after Kosinski, a penniless émigré, had arrived from Russia, through his right-wing books on economics, written under the pseudonym Joseph Novak. The marriage was of short duration.

"We were an ill-matched pair," he had mused. Yet when she died, he mourned and during her final illness, though divorced, he recalled that he lay on the floor outside her hospital room, "like a dog."

Was he grieving for the pretty, blond woman and her untimely death, or for her fortune, gained and lost? Perhaps both, and for a long time he treasured her memory, a Hope diamond in the iron vault of his mind, a casket stripped of the velvet cushioning of sentimentality.

Jerzy Kosinski, Katherina (Kiki) von Fraunhover (later to be his second wife), Carlos and Sylvia Fuentes, my husband and I were on holiday in Venice, an unreal city, a lovely bauble, unsubstantial, amnesiac, a beachcomber's paradise. Bedecked in decay, it is drowning, slowly, in the polluted waters of its canals. On this visit I was to share my vision with friends native to different parts of the old world (Carlos Fuentes and his wife, from Mexico City, Kiki von Fraunhover, a German, Kosinski, Polish); perhaps, through them at home in many places, I might solidify my view of Venice. When I explored churches, museums, palazzi, or crossed the expanse, great as a lake, of the Piazza San Marco with Carlos Fuentes, I had a cicerone who was, at once, an habitué and an erudite, curious foreigner. As for Jerzy Kosinski, he seemed to belong here, everywhere and nowhere.

On the last evening in Venice, we dined at the Hotel Cipriani, where Carlos and Sylvia were staying. Distanced by only meters of water from the main island, the hotel was an opposite world, with neither romance nor a past. A cheerful, luxurious, manicured resort, it had resisted the infection of art and decomposition situated nearby. The swimming pools, tennis courts, and flower gardens were well tended, related to their own type in every country. In the sumptuous dining room, one rich international course followed the next, each dish covered with a shining silver dome. We ate and drank heartily; only Jerzy was abstemious, barely wetting his thin lips on his Champagne glass and nibbling on a sliver of toast with smoked salmon. He required scant ordinary nourishment; his electric vitality was fed by some unknown source. That night, his discourse was sharp, abrasive, provocative, the ice-pellet words freezing even the brilliant conversation of Carlos Fuentes, who observed Kosinski with the attentiveness of the novelist always on the lookout for material that might, someday, be utilized for his works.

On the dock, Kiki, Jerzy, my husband, and I said good-bye to Carlos and Sylvia, promising to have a reunion soon, and we boarded the *vaporetto* for the brief return transit. Kosinski reclined among the pillows on the deck, but he did not relax; his body was an arrow ready to spring from a taut bow.

"The night has just begun for us," he said. "We usually

hire a gondola at this hour to explore the back *callies*. Along the way we pick up prostitutes, here, sailors, there, and they join us aboard. We amuse ourselves in various ways."

I pictured this *Walpurgisnacht* orgy: Kiki, Amazonian and practical, bent to her master's will. Now we were approaching Venice, its domes and towers rising abruptly out of the water. In the flickering light on the *vaporetto*, Kosinski's face had a compelling, eerie beauty, closed as a satanic mask worn by an eighteenth-century reveler at a ball in a Renaissance palazzo while it was still in full glory, before decay and threat of submersion. The evening at the Cipriani dwindled and vanished, consumed in a moment of timelessness against which the material is defenseless.

When we disembarked, Jerzy and Kiki moved off in one direction, we in another. For no apparent reason, I looked back just as Kosinski and his companion were disappearing through the door of their hotel. And the floating brothel, had it only been invented for our benefit, another tale to shock the bourgeoisie? I experienced an irrational disappointment, and, unexpectedly, a different scene out of my childhood returned to me. I was dining with my family at a French seaside resort, when my father announced that the Prince of Wales was sitting at the next table. Yet all I saw was an ordinary young man in golfing costume—no crown, no ermine-bordered velvet robe, no scepter. Long later, on a street in Venice, in my mind's eye, I followed Kosinski through the lobby, into the lift, down the corridor to his hotel room, along a route identical to the one I would be taking shortly.

Through the years, it seemed to me that Kosinski's oral sagas were altering, the gypsy being replaced by the Jewish survivor of the Holocaust. But in my view, he remained a loner, affiliated with no group, without any shared history, attached to his own book, *The Painted Bird*.

Now, he often acted as chairman, fund raiser, and orator for charitable events. He was effective as president of the American P.E.N. and on behalf of Amnesty International, and many a political prisoner might thank him for freedom. Introducing Eastern European literature in the United States became a mission and just as once a dedicated socialist evoked the name of Karl Marx, Kosinsky called upon Bruno Schulz, the late author, victim of the Nazis. One evening, from my place in an auditorium, I observed Kosinski on the podium, behind a microphone, delivering a money-raising speech for liberated Czechoslovakia. His voice was rasping, weaker, the words less staccato, but he appeared as stylish as ever. Yet like a ghost over his shoulder I saw a different figure: a Warsaw schoolboy, wearing an old-fashioned cap and an adult's overcoat, several sizes too large for him, from a pre-Holocaust photograph caught by the camera of Roman Vishnyac. Images of the ghetto population still unaware of its approaching fate, they break our hearts, and from our safe niche in place and time, we want to scream to warn those innocents arrested in suspended motion. The vision of the schoolboy faded and the renowned author stood alone on the stage.

I read in *The New York Times* the account of Jerzy Kosinski's macabre suicide. He was found dead, lying in his bathtub, his head bound inside a plastic shopping bag, his chosen implement for suffocation. I visualized his dark face showing through the transparent material, and it brought to mind the creations of the artist, Christo; the bridges of the river Seine wrapped in plastic shrouds, while the portentous stone gargoyles on the cathedral of Nôtre-Dame survey the scene, mutely. It was a shock to learn, later, that this way of taking one's life was not a final demonic gesture on the part of Jerzy Kosinsky, but the method recommended by the Hemlock Society. What cause had triggered his death? I remembered being told by a survivor that the burden of Holocaust memories never grows lighter and may, at any moment, become too heavy to endure. That arrogant presence who trod the ground so lightly, was he the product of his own tricks and my fancy? Did I, as a Jew, wish to invest one of my own kind with supernatural invincibility? During all those years had I overlooked a human being? In any case, I am certain that Jerzy Kosinski would have scorned compassion.

I hasten to reread *The Painted Bird*.

Chapter Eighteen

SINGER'S CITY

Who is crossing the wide avenue? He is of small stature, fair complexioned, and wears a long, dark winter coat, although it is spring and the weather is warm. He is over seventy, but he scuttles with the rapidity of a beetle. From under his felt hat his wide, pale blue eyes peer, as darting as his gait. And the tips of his large, flat ears are as pointed as a fawn's. He is clutching a brown paper bag. It is Isaac Singer.

When he reaches me, he bobs his head in an old-world bow. "I am not late, am I?" he asks. His English is flavored by a Yiddish accent, the same diction that lingers in his translated stories and novels, giving them the blended richness of a native brew. "I stopped on the way to buy some bird food," he says, holding out the paper bag. Singer has an affinity for birds. "They are God's creatures, too," he says. And he is a familiar sight on upper Broadway, scattering grain, in the company of a congregation of bedraggled city pigeons.

After lunch we walk up Broadway to West Eighty-sixth Street, where Singer lives. Our ritual does not vary: We always go to the Tiptoe Inn, where the cheesecake, blintzes, rice pudding, or stewed prunes I had watched Singer eating remind me of familiar details in his stories. When we leave we move quickly, and sometimes I am forced to break into a run to keep up with his scurrying pace. He is impatient now to reach home to begin his translation. On the way, he sometimes relates bits of a story he is working on: "It is called *The Son from America*. He returns to the little town in Poland where he was born. He wants to bestow his American money on his simple parents and the village people. But they do not know how to use his worldly gifts; they are contented to remain poor, chanting inside their synagogue, protected by their faith in God. "I will not tell you what happens at the end—you will soon hear it," Singer promises while I gallop at his side, as eager as he to get there.

Singer's apartment building is a relic constructed during the nineteenth century. Once a luxury building, the large, solid structure, enclosing a sunless courtyard, takes up an entire city block. Now somewhat shabby, it looks like a fortress or, perhaps, a converted prison. Singer once told me that he chose it because the courtyard reminded him of his childhood home on Krochmalna Street in Warsaw. We open a Bastille-like gate and cross the yard. Our footsteps echo; we are alone in the deserted area.

Outside his door he stoops to pick up his mail: Yiddish periodicals, magazines on extrasensory perception (he is an enthusiastic subscriber), and his fan letters. The interior is spacious: a long, obscure foyer, a living room, and a dining room furnished in the conventional style of the continental bourgeoisie by Alma, his wife, who came from Munich. Singer seems like a transient here. But two rooms, rarely visited, are particularly his own. The study where he composes is crammed with manuscripts and old newspapers. The disorder is only apparent, however; it is a sign of power, like the eye of a storm. In the bedroom two parakeets fly free: The door of their cage is always open. A male and a female, they look like enamel birds, electric blue and parrot green. But I know that they are poor substitutes for the original, Matzoth.

The story of Matzoth tells something significant but not definitive about Singer. One summer morning, as he was sitting at the kitchen table by the window open to the courtyard, he wished for a companion. Immediately, as if in answer, a parakeet flew inside. "As soon as I saw him, I knew we would be friends. God had sent him to me. He was an old soul." Matzoth would alight on Singer's bald pate, and Singer, holding very still and rolling his large, blue eyes upward, would converse with the bird in a special voice reserved just for him. "Say something, Matzoth," he would coax. "I am listening." The bird would chirp away. Seeing them like this, I could not help noticing their likeness: Singer's small, round head, with his pointed nose and wise eyes, was echoed in avian terms in Matzoth's tiny, aquiline profile and the uncanny intelligence of his expression. "Talk, Matzoth," Singer repeated and, turning to me, said, "No, don't go away; he is about to say something." As I waited, I leafed through the case history books on demonic possession and hallucination on Singer's desk. His stories are laced with demons, "dybbuks," and fiery kabbalistic angels. Singer's preoccupation with the spirit world is puzzling. Is he magician, bewitcher or bewitched, or both at once? There is a twinkle in his eye when he talks of these things, but he is serious also. It is better to smile than to shudder; for Singer, humor is the path to wisdom.

I recall the day that he and Alma came to visit us at our country home. It was a rare event, since Singer does not enjoy a bucolic environment; he is a man of the city and prefers his rapid walks along crowded streets. Whether observing an elegant boulevard or a shabby street, his penetrating eye is able to absorb humanity even as he flies past; trees, flowers, and grass only give him hay fever! But rural settings do occasionally appear in his stories; accurately observed but brief, they are little more than clouds that momentarily dim the probing light of his urban descriptions. The only landscape he knows well is Bilgoray, the Polish *shtetl* of a small East European market town, where his maternal grandfather, a "wonder rebbe," used to hold court. At our place Singer sat stiffly on the terrace in a straight-backed wrought-iron chair. He still obstinately wore his dark suit, a necktie, and heavy, polished black oxford shoes, although the rest of us lounged in sport shirts, slacks, and sandals. Despite his affinity with the dusty pigeons on Broadway and his own pet parakeets, he appeared indifferent to the crimson cardinals, golden orioles, wild canaries, and bluebirds that came to peck from our model glass feeder, swinging from a branch of a maple tree that flourished near the terrace. The vegetable garden, of which my husband is very proud, elicited scant praise from Singer: A heaping plate of cooked legumes surrounding a boiled potato is more to his taste. And neither our giant poodle (although he addressed him diffidently as "Brother Dog") nor our granddaughters tumbling over the newly mown lawn caught his attention. Then, unexpectedly, as if stimulated by a change of gears that brought about a deeper intensity, a livelier rhythm, Singer asked, "Well, and what about the ghost room?"

I remembered that we had told him about a room in our home that originally had been the study of Oscar Straus, my husband's grandfather; he had built this house for retirement for himself and his wife in their old age. We had turned the study into an extra bedroom, having discovered in the attic a Victorian bed so large that we judged that several generations of the family might have been spawned upon its broad, comfortable expanse. We also found a marble-topped night table and a Chinese lamp supported by two porcelain mandarins beneath a fringed shade, brittle as old parchment. We added heirloom photographs, and a lepidopterist friend had contributed a collection of butterflies and moths preserved under glass. The fragile, fading wings—

insect mummies—suited the special ambience of the room. But the major piece of furniture is a tall armoire. Wakeful, in the middle of the night, one is aware of a mysterious creaking, almost a groan, issuing from behind its closed doors. "You may hear Grandfather's ghost," we warn a guest who is about to occupy that room. It has become a standard remark, to me full of literary allusions. I envision the ghost of Hamlet's father mingling with the image of Grandfather, and our guest room is transformed into a domestic Elsinor.

Isaac Singer has a different attitude toward the world of phantoms. For him apparitions are real, not merely literary metaphors. He senses them all about: "Who knows?" he says. "Perhaps they have some message for us more important than the utterances we call rational of ordinary conversation!"

I took him upstairs, and he expressed the wish to be left alone. And, just as a fish liberated from the hook may be returned to the water, his natural medium, Isaac Singer disappeared into the musty "ghost room," relieved to be shed of the uncongenial "outdoors."

When he rejoined us on the terrace after what seemed a long time, my husband inquired in the offhand manner generally used by disbelievers when referring to things supernatural, "Well, Isaac, did you see Grandfather's ghost?" "No, I did not," he replied. Then he added wistfully, "You know that it is usually those who scoff at the idea of the existence of spirits who will most probably meet one. All of my life I have searched for them, but so far, I have had no success."

He fixed the x-ray beam of his blue eyes upon an editor from my husband's firm who was also visiting us. Hal was a dapper man, erect, with a neat toothbrush mustache and a clipped manner of speech. Cosmopolitan and intellectually sophisticated, he had spent some time in Paris on the fringes of the Hemingway-Stein set. With the assurance of an oracle announcing the demise of a decadent civilization, Singer addressed him. "For instance, you, my friend—you, who do not believe in such foolish things—will probably meet a ghost some day. While I, just because I know they are there, will never see one. They will go on hiding from me. But I will not stop trying—I will hope, anyway."

Singer has never returned to try his luck in the "ghost room" again. But since that time, whenever I hear creaks and groans in the wardrobe, instead of being reminded of the ghost of Hamlet's father—pale and silver bearded, with a king's crown upon his head—I see, quite clearly, Oscar Straus. He wears a panama hat, and on the sleeve of his summer jacket there is a broad, black mourning band commemorating the death of a now forgotten kinsman. Although he is old, his beard is fiery red; it is the color of Isaac Singer's hair when he was young.

At Singer's apartment on Broadway, Matzoth continues to peep. At last Singer announces, "He has spoken." "What did he say?" "Case history," Singer answers. With a smile and a shrug he releases me, and the bird flies off its perch on the domed forehead. "There are more things in this world than you and I can understand," Singer says.

A few years after Matzoth's sudden appearance, he disappeared on another hot summer morning. In spite of the heat, it had been ordered that the windows should always remain shut when Matzoth was loose, but on this day Alma had been careless, for the window on the courtyard had been left open, and through it Matzoth departed as abruptly as he had entered. Frantic, Singer placed notices in the newspapers, searched the streets, the roof, inquired of neighbors, but Matzoth had vanished forever. "It was God's will. He came and he went." But he could not conceal his grief. "These two," he would say about the replacement, "are foolish creatures." The frivolous pair would dart about the bedroom, pecking here, perching there, clinging with the twiglike claws to the ceiling, heads downward. "They are not old souls like Matzoth," said Singer.

Singer takes off his overcoat, hangs it in the closet in the foyer, and scurries to his armchair in the living room, from which he dictates his translations from the original manuscript of *The Jewish Daily Forward*, where his works always appear first in print. I sit on the striped sofa with a pad on my knees, and I scramble, as on our walks, to keep pace with him. My role is that of a grammarian, changing the tense of a verb or altering its position. Occasionally, he calls upon me to improve his English rendering of a Yiddish word, for which small service I am disproportionately thanked. When he misplaces a page, he rummages through his pockets as scraps of paper covered with his fine, old-fashioned script flutter to the floor, copious and free as snowflakes. "Ah! I have found it," he exclaims as he resettles his spectacles on the high bridge of his nose. "These papers have a way of opposing me."

At intervals during a session he jumps up to answer the telephone: a confirmation of a lecture engagement or yet another admirer. He returns to his armchair, and the dictation is resumed as though there had been no interruption; his concentration is continuous. And in his work his vision makes Jewish life whole, all contradictions included: the Old World and the New World, the Torah and the Kabbalah, the saintly and the swinish.

I can still remember the first story he translated in my presence. It was called "Henne Fire," and its subject was a witchlike woman, dark and emaciated as a charred bone. She was an incendiary who caused flames to spring up wherever she might be. Singer told me that when he was ten years old, he had glimpsed the model for this fictional creature through a keyhole view into the court of his father, the rabbi. He had kept it in the storehouse of memory, to be used some fifty years later. But from the prominent, sharp eyes of the adult the small boy curiously peers out, and what the child learned in his father's court the man proclaims today. Through the many strands of his tales runs a dominating obsession: The way of life carried on in the ghettos of Eastern Europe must never be forgotten.

So we sit close together and far apart. We are like remote cousins with contrasting nationalities and family customs: the son and grandson of pious Hasidic rabbis from Poland and the New York City Jew of German descent, atheistically reared, brought up on the ideal of the "melting pot" and the hope of eventual assimilation. Singer and I never cease to marvel inwardly at our differences at the same time that we recognize our kinship.

Through the years the stories proliferate. Place names, though I am still unable to pronounce them, are like old friends: Rejowiec, Shidlovtse, Radom, Kielce, Krasnobrod, Bilgoray. Alien characters have grown familiar: Yentl; Beyle; Meir, the eunuch; Zalman, the glazier; Zeinl; Zeitz; Itche Godl; Getsl; Bendit Pupko.

Mrs. Pupko's beard: the picture on the television screen comes into focus, a reduced mirror image of "a day in the life of Isaac Bashevis Singer." There is upper Broadway, the asphalt islands, the restless vehicles, the diverse humans, the pigeons, the cafeterias. And there is Singer's fortresslike apartment building with its deserted court-yard and, inside, the rooms of his home: the living room, the wildly disordered study filled with the records of his imagination. Included among the familiar things and people reproduced by the shifting pictures on the television screen is a fantastic figure: "a woman dressed in a shabby black dress, man's shoes and hat, with a white beard." It is Mrs. Pupko out of Singer's story, "The

Beard." Bruce Davidson, the filmmaker, has succeeded in combining a literal documentary and one of Singer's most grotesquely enigmatic tales.

The ten-page story that says so much in so few lines opens in a Broadway cafeteria where seedy Yiddish authors gather to talk about literature, success, and money. One of the group, Bendit Pupko, has somehow become a rich man and has bribed a critic to write a favorable essay on his work. Over their "rice puddings" and "egg cookies," the others discuss the scandal. The narrator vows to Bendit Pupko that *he* cannot be bought. Soon after, he receives a visit from Pupko's wife, who has loved her husband and been loved by him for over forty years. She is a conjugal Isolde, but much to the narrator's astonishment she sports a flourishing beard! In response to his questioning, Mrs. Pupko tells him that Bendit has always found her beard (now white, once black) alluring, and he would not permit her to shave it off. No, he is not a homosexual or anything of the kind. Although the beard had brought her loneliness and virtual isolation, Mrs. Pupko complied with her husband's wishes. "People have idiosyncrasies that can't be explained. Nu," she says, "one mustn't know everything." The narrator is moved by Mrs. Pupko's entreaties to give her husband a good review. But Bendit Pupko dies before it appears in print. Several years later the narrator meets Mrs. Pupko sitting alone in a neighborhood automat. He is dismayed to see that the beard is still there. "Why? since her husband is now dead," he wants to ask. But he remembers her words, "Nu, one must not know everything."

In Bruce Davidson's film I was given a bit part representing Singer's "translators." Pen and pad in hand, I was placed outside his front door. I felt self-conscious and nervous as I rang the bell. Just as in real life, Singer greeted me with old-world courtesy and haste to begin his work. He sat down in the same armchair; I, on the striped sofa. And he insisted that he would not "pretend." He did not wish to waste time; he would actually translate a story while the scene was being filmed. The strong lights made me uncomfortable, the camera crew was a distraction, and I followed the dictation haltingly. Outside the window on Broadway a fire engine siren screeched. "Cut," Davidson commanded, and I was obliged to go behind the door again, to ring the bell once more, to make another entrance. Singer, used to interruptions, took up the story where he had left off. His voice was even and natural. But at another order from Davidson, the cameras halted once more. "What is it now?" asked Singer. "Defective lighting," the filmmaker answered. Singer shrugged, and I disappeared another time. Although the procedure was repeated again and again, I could not lose my stiffness nor the awareness that I was acting a part. Singer, annoyed by the delays, managed to get on with the translation, and he appeared as much at ease as when we were alone on an ordinary afternoon.

When I viewed the completed scene on the screen, I was amazed at its brevity. So many retakes, so much equipment for an episode that was over almost before it had begun. I was embarrassed by my own air of theatricality and admired Singer's naturalness in this episode and throughout the film. We see him in his long overcoat, with a paper bag in his hand, feeding the pigeons on Broadway, meeting the *landsleit* in a cafeteria, sprinting around his courtyard, having breakfast with Alma, arriving at the office of the *Jewish Daily Forward*—and always he is just as we know him. But he is most himself when he confronts the actor (the only professional in the film) who plays Mrs. Pupko. Then, at once the bewitcher and the bewitched, he encounters the materialized monster of his own creation, with a mixture of horrified incredulity and philosophical acceptance.

And we know that the thought spoken by Mrs. Pupko is his own, "Nu, one must not know everything."

In his living room, when Singer puts aside his manuscript or a serialized version of a story in the *Forward*, I ask, "How does it end?"

"You will see," he answers. I beg to know now what will happen. I have become the listener of old; Singer, the proverbial storyteller. "Wait," he repeats, "you will know what happens next time."

The session is over for today. My fingers are cramped, but I would like more. When I descend into the courtyard, it is still deserted. But in my fancy it has broken into seething activity: The Yeshiva boys, the shopkeepers, the glaziers, the midwives, the women on their way to the ritual bath, the town gossips, the lechers, the beadles, all jostle one another, and the air is filled with the expressive singsong of the Yiddish language. From a balcony of his home, the rabbi's little boy surveyed such a scene, and the memory of it empowers Isaac Singer to populate an empty quadrangle with the vanished life of the Warsaw ghetto. I pass through the Bastille-like gate, and the harsh reality of Broadway appears to be a dream.

When I reach the agora of Columbus Circle, the woman is stationed, as usual, at the entrance to Central Park. Around her the streets fan out into a kaleidoscope, with the statue of Christopher Columbus on his pedestal at the center. People dwarfed by the sudden opening of the city are moving in every direction, oblivious to the newspaper headlines displayed in front of a kiosk; the billboard advertising overhead; the angry honking and zig-zagging of cars; and the strange woman who exhorts them endlessly from her habitual post, with her back to the green peace of the park. Her lecture is muffled by some young street musicians and, nearby, a vendor is exhibiting his mechanical toys; their jerky animation imitates the crowd of pedestrians who cross Columbus Circle.

It has been my custom to walk quickly past this woman, and just as one might avert one's eyes from the sight of a street accident, I used to avoid looking at the bizarre irrationality of her performance. But today, for some reason, I pause and take careful note of her appearance. She is middle-aged, tall, husky, with a broad face and a ruddy complexion. Is it due to drink or long hours in the open air? Her sandy hair is drawn into a ponytail, and she wears a shabby, brown winter coat. She might be taken for a rural schoolteacher, except for the fact that her legs, like wintering shrubs, are bound in burlap rags. For the first time I try to distinguish the words she pretends to be reading from the blank sheet she holds in her hands: "in as much . . . and heretofore . . . in order that . . . in terms of . . . hopefully, at this point in time . . ." The gibberish is repeated over and over. There is nothing else, but the tone is reasonable, calm, patiently explanatory. Perhaps, the "dybbuk" of a dead statesman is struggling to make itself heard through the lips of this woman, I think to myself, as I hear Isaac Singer saying, "There are more things in this world than you and I can understand." For the moment, the sorcerer has given me his eyes and ears.

Chapter Nineteen

LITTLE COLETTE

Large cities are composed of enclaves, as though to mitigate their overwhelming size and the awesome longevity of stone, asphalt, and iron. And just as a celebrity may assume in society a deceptive air of bonhomie, the streets of Paris intersected by boulevards and architectural vistas, are made intimate by quarters resembling French salons. Door, windows, balconies, patios are like period furnishings, witness to successions of urban gatherings. They bring the past nearer and endow my transitory visits to Paris with keyhole glimpses into history.

For a time, shortly after World War II, I liked to linger in the courtyard of the Palais Royal. Beneath its arcades, I seemed to recover a faint cacophony of faraway voices: French Revolutionary orators as well as farmers from outlying districts, shopkeepers, prostitutes, and money lenders hawking their wares. Now the area is deserted and silent except for the occasional shouts of children at play.

The Palace, enclosing three sides of the quadrangle, is as extensive as a Renaissance town. It had been built in the seventeenth century by Louis XIII, for Cardinal Richelieu, but it was Anne of Austria who became its first tenant. With the rise of the bourgeoisie, the royal suites were transformed into a community of apartment complexes. I was always drawn to a particular window, no different from its neighbors, but on the wall beneath the regulation balcony where ordinary city sparrows hopped and twittered, a brass plaque was inscribed: *Colette lived here.*

The sight of ancient places may be markers for the past, but books, also, are beacons along the route of the years. For me, for a long time, the works of Colette shone steadily. Yet, although my husband became her publisher and we promised one another that we would make the pilgrimage to the current reigning literary royalty of the Palais Royal, we never did so. And I saw her only with my imagination, at the end of her life, crippled by arthritis, confined, for the most part, to the ship of her famous king-size bed in her apartment in the Palais Royal. From there, she continued to write with gnarled fingers and to receive friends and their offerings of flowers, choice chocolates, or a bag of chestnuts with rough, hairy shells that recaptured her childhood in Provence. To her sensitive nostrils, olfactory antennae, the products of nature were aromatic as any perfume. In her painful immobility she could be consoled, also, by the velvety padded touch of a cat, or the soft, voluptuous folds of an afghan. An aged great lady, a hedonist, she continued to sport a tousled head of curls and a coquettish, frizzy belle époque bang, beneath which her feline glance retained all of its cunning acuteness. But she died before I could behold her in actuality.

I had her books. Most of her novels are set in Paris, the scene of her adult life: on the stages of music halls and theatres, in the feminine world of the demi-monde. She moved among the famous writers and performers of her day. A lover of her own sex, Colette was able to enjoy men, as well; in late middle age, she would claim that the flesh of her young lover was as seductive as the downy skin of a peach.

The work that I chose to read and reread is a memoir of her childhood in the village of Saint Sauver in Provence, light-years removed from the bohemian sophistications of Paris. The central figure is a woman, Colette's mother, an icon garlanded with the produce of the earth, and by small country creatures: field mice, rabbits, lizards, birds, and butterflies, the composition painted in vibrant words, bathed in the mellow light of loving recollection.

But deception is buried somewhere. Just like those puzzle picture games from my childhood, in which a face was concealed in the foliage of a tree, these buoyant memories mask a vein of longing and deprivation. The title—*My Mother's House*—is telltale. The home belongs to Her: Sido (Sidonie), and the boisterous children surrounding her resemble the small animals decorating the rustic goddess of the icon. As for the father, with his wooden leg (a trophy from World War I), he is scarcely more interesting to his daughter than an old carriage horse sequestered in his stable library.

"I follow her vaguely disturbed that she [Sido] should be worrying about my father. . . . he scarcely ever goes out, she knows perfectly well where he is. There would have been more sense, for instance, had she said to me 'Minet-Chéri, you're looking pale. Minet-Chéri, what's the matter?' "[6]

Although Sido remained an oddly elusive parent, all things existed to worship her—the mother—the supreme invention of her daughter, the writer Colette. Sido was more attuned to Nature than to any person.

". . . Already out of sight, her voice still reached us, a brisk soprano voice full of inflexions that trembled at the slightest emotion and proclaimed to all and sundry news of delicate

[6] *My Mother's House*, Farrar, Straus, Giroux, 1953 & 1993.

plants, of gratings, of rain and blossomings, like the voice of a hidden bird that foretells the weather . . . "[7]

Surely, the child might have wished for something more, and occasionally, her need broke through the artist's pigment of idolatry, but it was quickly covered over by another layer of rich paint. The adolescent Colette watches her mother mend a broken vine, binding it around twenty times with gold string.

". . . I shivered and thought it was with jealousy," she wrote, "but it was merely a poetic echo awakened in me by the magic of that effective aid sealed in gold."[8]

In her memoir, personal longings are transformed into a matriarchal mythology, and I, perhaps foolishly, wanted to meet the founder of this pagan faith. Books, however, should be kept separate from their makers, but just like a lover who courts domesticity, not realizing that familiarity will extinguish the glow of romance, we continue to seek out the flesh and blood human who has already given us the best of himself on the printed page.

Eventually, however, I did penetrate that special apartment above the entrance to the courtyard of the Palais Royal. But it was, merely, ordinary, dark, and cramped, permeated by the smell of cabbage being cooked next door. Colette de Jouvenel (known as "Little Colette" to distinguish her name from her famous mother's) was our guide, pointing out this, explaining that. Everything had been left reverently in place, exactly as it used to be. For the guardian of this museum—domicile—each homely object represented a relic in a shrine. We followed Little Colette over the premises, the rooms the ailing, aged writer had called home for her last years. I paused longest near the bed from which the arcades at the Palace could be viewed when the heavy

[7] *My Mother's House*, Farrar, Straus, Giroux.
[8] *My Mother's House*, Farrar, Straus, Giroux, 1953 & 1993.

window drapes were parted. But with the disappearance of its occupant, the legendary "barge-couch" was just another shabby piece of furniture, and the "blue lantern" was merely a goose-necked lamp. In the kitchen, however, the utensils appeared to have been put aside only yesterday: the knives, forks, and spoons at readiness for use, a pottery bowl, though empty, held the shadow of piled fruits and those rare hairy chestnuts indigenous to the region of Provence. I thought of the Etruscan tombs in which the deceased are buried along with their household artifacts to keep them company in the realm of death. In Colette's apartment, on the contrary, these domestic articles were preserved for the benefit of the living—the admirers of the renowned author. But they served only to emphasize her death and the perishability of humans in contrast to the permanence of inanimate objects.

A large photograph of a handsome, fair-haired man caught my eye.

"My father," Colette de Jouvenel explained.

This portrait must have been a posthumous addition to the museum. Surely, Colette had not lived with the likeness of her divorced husband. In her life, as in her books, Henri de Jouvenel had glided almost imperceptibly. His countenance was a jarring note in this feminine cave of remembrance. Furthermore, I could discover no trace of family likeness in his daughter's plain face.

As she displayed with pride her mother's abandoned possessions, I examined her carefully. The genes are often capricious—could this middle-aged, weathered woman, dressed in dowdy country tweeds, wearing sensible ground-gripper ox-ford shoes, be the offspring of the correctly good-looking de Jouvenel and Colette? Had she ever been that child-sprite, "Bel-Gazou" (her mother's pet name for her), known to us from the memoirs? Rather, she resembled a French version of Miss

Marple, the mannish British heroine of Agatha Christie's mystery novels.

"This is my mother's shawl," she was saying.

But I shrank from the gossamer wrap, as though it had been a shroud.

A light rain was falling outside in the courtyard where the treble voices of children were proclaiming the scorings of their game of ball. I wished to escape into the semi-open air of the roofless quadrangle.

"Where should we go for lunch?" my husband asked.

"When I am in Paris I always dine in the Palais Royal, at the restaurant Grand VeFour. They reserve my mother's table for me," Colette de Jouvenel answered. And, grabbing her oversized, serviceable, mannish black umbrella, she preceded us down the dark narrow stairs, as accompanied by the persistent smell of cabbage, we left the apartment.

"Wait for me here, I'll be right back. I must fetch my little dog," Colette called, as she trotted out of sight.

Beneath the balcony of the writer's apartment, the words engraved on the brass plaque had lost their import.

The restaurant Grand VeFour nestles within the historic compound of the Palais Royal. Many generations of famous diners have come and gone, as well as the anonymous imprint of a child tourist in Paris—that other self that I used to be in the company of my father, an enthusiastic gourmet. As my eyes grew accustomed to the twilight in the temple devoted to culinary art, a host of nymphs in scanty draperies bearing cornucopias overflowering with fruits and flowers emerged painted on the glass panels of the halls. Years later, they are still there; they still offer up their bounty to the senses just as in a cathedral the saints depicted on stained glass pay homage to the soul.

The maître d' greeted Colette de Jouvenel with ceremony and led us to her mother's special table in a corner of the room. Dressed in swallowtails and pin-striped trousers, he might have been a red-robed cardinal officiating in the false night of a cathedral. As I slid along the banquette, making room for Little Colette and Sasha, her miniature brown poodle, I felt like the boy Marcel Proust, had he been privileged to enter the aristocratic, historic pew of the Duchesse de Guermantes in the church at Combray.

After a deep bow, the waiter, carrying a menu large as a map of the world, withdrew. Colette had ordered white truffles. "My mother's favorite dish," she told us, adding that Colette used to say that they prepared them here, just as Sido used to do.

Sasha, seated between his mistress and me, was daintily picking at the smoked salmon on her plate.

"I like it here," Colette de Jouvenel commented, "they truly appreciate dogs."

Yet I sensed that our hostess was eager to return to her home in the country. But the site was not Saint Sauver, with its luxuriant southern fertility. Rather, I pictured her striding over the sandy, barren hillocks of Normandy, her tweed cape billowing in a salt, north wind. She is followed by a pack of sporting dogs and the citified dandy, Sasha, her constant companion on her brief stays in Paris. The obscure rural existence must have been a lonely one, lived in the shadow of her mother, and it was her renown that brought Little Colette to the city (an awkward, middle-aged vestal virgin), to tend the altar to literary fame.

I had heard, often, people murmuring, "Poor little Colette, she never had a real mother!" It was true that motherhood was not natural to Colette, who entrusted the care of her "Bel Gazou" to a governess, while she led her uninterrupted Parisian life away from the salubrious seaside nursery of her only child. On brief visits, she played the mother role, a classical actress declaiming her love in self-conscious poetic phrases. Now I see Colette de Jouvenel walking alone. Overhead, the gulls seem to be calling, "Bel-*Gazou, Bel-Gazou*," but the name repeated by the birds is cold—distant as the whitecaps on the horizon of a gray, northern ocean.

We parted from our hostess outside the restaurant Grand VeFour. In my last view of Little Colette, she is standing in a heavy rain with Sasha, her miniature poodle, held closely like a cherished baby in her arms, sheltered from the downpour by the oversized, black, utilitarian umbrella.

Behind her, through the sooty fog, the image of the other Colette loomed! The Parisian author, woman of the world, with her trademark thatch of curly hair, her clever feline glance, beneath the frivolous *Belle Epoque* bang. Mother and daughter are joined in a double exposure of the insufficiently loved child.

COLOPHON

Dorothea Straus is the author of six other books including *Virgins and Other Endangered Species* (Moyer Bell). She lives in New York City.

This book was typeset by Alabama Book Composition, Deatsville, Alabama. The text was set in Adobe Garamond, a typeface designed by Claude Garamond (c. 1500-61). The display faces are Bernhard Fashion and Nuptial Script.

The Paper Trail was printed by
Thomson-Shore, Inc., Dexter, Michigan
on acid free paper.